THE GARDEN THAT I LOVE, SECOND SERIES

THE GARDEN THAT I LOVE, SECOND SERIES

Alfred Austin

www.General-Books.net

Publication Data:

Title: The Garden That I Love, Second Series
Author: Austin, Alfred, 1835-1913
Publisher: London : Macmillan and co., limited
Publication date: 1907

How We Made This Book for You
We made this book exclusively for you using patented Print on Demand technology.
First we scanned the original rare book using a robot which automatically flipped and photographed each page.
We automated the typing, proof reading and design of this book using Optical Character Recognition (OCR) software on the scanned copy. That let us keep your cost as low as possible.
If a book is very old, worn and the type is faded, this can result in typos or missing text. This is also why our books don't have illustrations; the OCR software can't distinguish between an illustration and a smudge.
We understand how annoying typos, missing text or illustrations, foot notes in the text or an index that doesn't work, can be. That's why we provide a free digital copy of most books exactly as they were originally published. Simply go to our website (www.general-books.net) to check availability. And we provide a free trial membership in our book club so you can get free copies of other editions or related books.
OCR is not a perfect solution but we feel it's more important to make books available for a low price than not at all. So we warn readers on our website and in the descriptions we provide to book sellers that our books don't have illustrations and may have typos or missing text. We also provide excerpts from each book to book sellers and on our website so you can preview the quality of the book before buying it.
If you would prefer that we manually type, proof read and design your book so that it's perfect, simply contact us for the cost. We would be happy to do as much work as you would be like to pay for.

THE GARDEN THAT I LOVE, SECOND SERIES

TO THE GENTLE READER

You may perhaps have observed that, whenever the author of l The Garden That I Love ' feels himself in a difficulty, he invariably has recourse either to Veronica, to whom he assigns his more romantic, or to the Poet whom he makes responsible for his more prosaic observations, but most of all to me, who am expected to pose in every imaginable attitude for his convenience. Having gradually become, by long maltreatment, steeped in sufferance, I have submitted to it all; and now he appeals to me afresh, and begs me to put on what he calls my most engaging manner, in order to propitiate all gentle readers, and to persuade you to tolerate a continuation or sequel to the volume by which he first became known to you. He is observant enough to be aware that striking the rock twice is, as a rule, rather a useless performance, but is pleased to believe, or at any rate to urge, that I have a special divining rod of my own, and can turn on a stream of interest from unsuspected sources.

Yes, it is to me he has recourse, when he is in a difficulty, and when I am in a difficulty, I seek relief from the Poet, and have accordingly done so on the present occasion. Never at a loss for an indulgent, or, as Veronica would say, a conscienceless, excuse for everything and everybody, he remarks, c seems to me, my dear, that hardly anything was ever said more untrue than that there is nothing new under the sun."

4 uite so," I replied, unable to resist the temptation, ' there is nothing new, except the old."' 1 That is one way of putting it," he resumed, in the same tolerant tone, 1 and perhaps as good a way as any. The old that is really good and great is always new, and the new that is bad or mediocre is old the day after it is born. One sometimes hears it said that a subject has been done to death. Then bring it to life again, if you can, by breathing into it your own personality, your mind, heart, and soul."' 1 But if you have not got any of these, and are destitute of personality," I objected, ' as indeed most people are? '

Then they must not waste time in flogging dead horses' 1 Is not that my unfortunate case? ' asked.

I shall not record his reply, being much too modest to do so, but will content myself with saying that it was ' just like him' But, having got to the end of his too partial favour for the questioner, he went on, ' Moreover, after the lapse of a dozen or so years, the same thing is no longer the same thing. Nothing remains or can remain stationary. Oneself has become more or less somebody else; and the Garden that we love, and its infatuated adorers, must also have changed in the interval. So, if it ever was worth seeing, you may depend on its being worth seeing still; and if what was written about it last century was worth reading, it will bear being written about in this. " The Odyssey" like every great poem, is just as new to-day as though it had Jirst appeared yesterday morning, while the popular novel of a decade ago is now unreadable. So that one comes round to your first observation that there is little which is new, except the old, the old that was at its birth really good." 1

Of course, if the Poet had been the author of ' The Garden That I Love," he could not have made this last observation. I sometimes wonder who was, and from time to time flatter myself that I wrote it. But then, as some indiscreet persons, I am told, have asked, Who is Lamia f Am I anything more than the Poet's dream? If 1 could only persuade myself of that, I should be perfectly happy.

Meanwhile, dear gentle reader, be, if possible, more gentle than ever, and come and see our really retired and retiring home whenever you feel disposed. If you are exceptionally respectable, Veronica, with her inexhaustible good nature, will take you round. If you have a lively sense of humour, tempered by occasional ebullitions, not too prolonged, of romantic sentiment, to me will fall the honour of being your guide and companion. If you have the good fortune to be comely to look on, or very attractive, it is just possible that the Poet himself will, quite accidentally, make his appearance, and saunter with you in its shadiest places. Even then, I shall not be far off.

LAMIA.

The Longest Day. Some too partial persons have been pleased to say that not only the writing of books concerning gardens, but the growing affection for them, owes something to The Garden that I Love. I am so little of an author, though so much of a gardener in a small way, that I fear the expression of this belief gives one a certain amount of pleasure, since even the most unambitious persons have, in their hearts, the foible of self-complacency as much as the most soaring. But this weakness receives its corrective from Lamia's irony and the Poet's chastening sense.

That you were first in the field," she says, in what I once called horticultural literature, I remember your saying in a moment of self-pluming, which I have noticed is common to neglected writers. But even the vanity of authorship cannot disguise from you that, though you may have learnt some- thing since then, you were rather a novice in horticulture when you first wrote on the subject, and that, in all which makes the true expert, you have been utterly outstripped since by some of your successors, who have towered high above your shoulders. Moreover, if I am to sit in the judgment-seat, and administer equity all round, you would cut a sorry figure among the writers of Garden Books, strictly so called, had it not been for the verses interspersed through your work, and which I yes, I procured for you, and which the writers, whom you would like to think your successors, have considerately abstained from imitating."

I always listen to Lamia's chastening humour, even when indulged at my expense, with unqualified pleasure, for, in truth, I am infatuated enough to like listening to anything she says, or watching anything she does; and more followed, to the same effect. But, conscious that there should be, as in all things, a limit to what has been called the Literature of Egotism, I will desist from reproducing more of the sort on that subject.

The Poet's observations on the matter amounted in substance to pretty much the same thing as Lamia's gossamer persiflage.

What is Priority? Somebody must speak first, in this reserved English world; and then everybody's tongue gradually gets loosened. We are all indebted to some one, indeed to many another. We have heard much, in our time, of self-made men; but I venture to say there can be no such thing, now that there have been on the earth so many generations of mankind, as a self-made man. Forgive me if I once again plead for what I have more than once called the Parent Past. No man nowadays can possibly be only himself, since there is in him no little of his father and mother, grandfathers and grandmothers, great-great-grandfathers and their wives, to say nothing of spiritual godfathers and godmothers, the Hebrew Prophets, Saint Luke, Saint Paul, Homer, Hesiod, Theocritus, Virgil, Dante, Chaucer, Shakespeare, and the rest, who were, so to speak, at our christening, and have given us much more than a silver mug and spoon, or to vary the metaphor, were our foster-parents almost from the first, and helped us from their capacious springs of life and health to grow in grace and strength. Let no one pique himself on absolute originality, for in truth there is no such thing, save of the wrong sort, which perhaps abounds overmuch in these novelty- demanding days, but, rather, humbly render thanks if we have been able to make a slight contribution towards the Present and the Future, in return for all we have inherited from the Past."

Veronica listened intently, for she likes her poet best in these equitable moments, having a hearty distaste for anything approaching to self-laudation. ' May I endorse, dear," she adds, ' every word of what you have been saying? Even Coriolanus must have been wrong when he exclaimed, "Alone I did it! " ' Is not the foregoing just? Books, all books, all good books at least, like all good gardens, owe much to people who did not actually create them. People living and dead, things past and present, all are contributories to that diminutive stream, oneself; a reflection which is essentially consoling, since it associates one with the sum of things, and prevents one from living in barren isolation. It has the further advantage of confirming the

Poet's favourite admonition, ' Repress your antipathies, cultivate your sympathics." I have found that piece of advice very helpful in regard to gardens, though one must not be so excessively tolerant as not to allow that there are some bad, very bad, even insufferably bad gardens; and these are, for the most part, gardens on which money has been lavishly expended. We were all much gratified on hearing from an amiable lady that, in our absence, she had asked a high dignitary of the Church who paid the garden that we love the compliment of coming to see it, what it was that made its charm, and that he replied, ' Obviously, Mind." I think he might have added, ' and Heart." I understand him to have meant that somebody's thoughts, somebody's root-principles in Art and taste in colour, had co-operated in its creation, and still presided over its existence. But, without the adjunct of heart, or Love, all the Mind in the world is powerless to produce the result that attracts and enthralls. Not only one must take pains with a thing, one must take pleasure in it as well. Bad gardens are either mindless, or heartless, or both. I am not talking of flowers, even the finest flowers. That demands but little thinking, and no loving whatever. There is no more difficulty in having splendid-looking rose-blooms, or huge carnations, than in growing giant beetroot or colossal potatoes. But that is not gardening. Magical gardening is quite another matter.

And now for a hazardous avowal. No prize-craving specimens have ever been sent hence to a Flower Show, either national or local. But we say among ourselves that if any one will offer a prize for the most satisfying garden, week after week and month after month, from, say, St. Valentine's Day to the close of Saint Luke's summer, the garden that we love will enter for the competition, and take its chance. We do not mean that it will be adjudged the Prize, but that the conditions are such as the lovers of gardens, as distinct from mere growers of flowers, though of course good gardening includes and embraces these, can cheerfully accept and abide by. I know nothing more misleading to the novice in gardening than Horticultural Shows, whether held at Holland House, in the Temple Gardens, or in any less famous spot. He will see there the most astonishingly perfect flowers, but will not know how much careful coddling they have undergone, what merciless disbudding, in many instances, there has been, and how many secondary blooms have been sacrificed in order to produce a prize-securing effect at one given moment. The flowers themselves are lovely to look at; but neither the means employed, nor the end attained, is gardening; nor will they enable any one to have a garden rightly so called.

The above opinion elicited from the Poet one of his philosophic reflections: ' I suppose," he said, ' perfection, like other good things, is to be attained only at a price, and the price is the sacrificing of something less perfect, for which, withal, perhaps on account of our own imperfection, we cannot help craving."

Does not the same thing, as you yourself have more than once explained," asked Lamia, ' hold good of Literature, alike in verse and prose? As regards what people still seem, in the abstract, to regard as the finest flower of Literature, namely Poetry, there are the two schools of opinion, two camps of taste and preference, the one insisting on the most painstaking execution possible, and the absence of anything like blot or blemish, the other inclining to a broader treatment and less finished style; or say, the artistically wrought detail of Tennyson, and the negligent grandeur of Byron. For more than a generation the former has been in favour with the majority of readers, though perhaps there are some signs of that preference declining."

Whenever Lamia talks seriously, Veronica only too willingly contributes to the conversation, and so observed, when Lamia ceased, 'Would it not be interesting to inquire what these recurring oscillations of taste and preference depend on? In respect of what Lamia has been suggesting, I am disposed to suspect that the explanation is to be sought in the circumstance whether the age happens to be mainly masculine or predominantly feminine in character, whether it be a stormy, seething, and tumultuous time, or one of comparatively placid airs and unruffled waters. Byron is as masculine in his writings as a poet well can be; for, in addition to his own tempestuous character, he lived in a time of electric skies, stormful flashes, and incessant thunder-peals. With what instantaneous sincerity, with what masculine recklessness, he gave expression to both! Quotation will best illustrate one's meaning:

Could I embody and unbosom now That which is most within me, could I wreak My thoughts upon expression, and thus throw Soul, heart, mind, passions, feelings, strong or weak, All that I would have sought, and all I seek, Bear, know, feel, and yet breathe, into one word, And that one word were lightning, I would speak.

In the same longing to identify and incorporate himself with stress and tumult, he exclaims, when describing the thunderstorm in the Alps at night

A sharer in thy fierce and far delight, A portion of the tempest and of thee!

There one has the whole man, or, rather, the whole Poet, unveiled. He seeks for one word, one concentrated aspect and operation of Nature, in which to embody and wherein to mirror himself; and he finds it in the word Lightning. Again, how he discloses himself, and reflects the period in which he lived and wrote, with its furibund tides and clashing waves, when he writes

Once more upon the waters! Yet once more! And the waves bound beneath me as a steed That knows its rider! Welcome to their roar! Swift to their guidance, wheresoe'er they lead!

They rejoice him all the more as the freshening sea makes them a terror; and he exultingly says of the ocean I am, as it were, a child of thee.

How could such a Poet concern himself overmuch to ask if this flashing wave of thought was kempt and curled to its very fringe and spray, or if that hurricane of feeling was as measured and musical as a cadence of Mozart."

I thought it was very praiseworthy in Veronica to express herself thus, for her own taste in literature, and above all in poetry, inclines to the greatest finish, and is averse to the hit-or-miss style of some writers; and I could see it gave the Poet pleasure to hear what she had just been saying.

I can imagine," he observed, nothing more true than what Veronica has just been urging. But I should like to add a word in favour of a theory of my own, such as it is, that, though probably no writer can wholly escape the influence of the age in which he happens to live, I doubt if that influence will be of much help or advantage to him unless it be in harmony with his own temperament. The more he yields to it, unless it be congenial to him, the more he sacrifices of himself; and to be oneself, in writing as in anything else, is to give one the best chance, not of popularity, but of doing the best work, and the best sort of work, for which one is by nature endowed. The Man does

not necessarily chime with the Hour. But, in Byron's case, the Man and the Hour met
to perfection. The age in
THE GARDEN THAT I LOVE n which he lived was very like himself in most
respects, and he resembled in essentials the age in which he lived. You may be born
out of your own time; and, in that case, you may, if weak and yielding, be reduced
to silence, or, if strong and with abundant power of resistance, have to wait for the
chance of some future age being more in agreement with you. Macaulay says that
Byron would have been a popular writer in any age. I venture to doubt that. Had
he been born so as to arrive at manhood, say, about the time of the first Reform Bill,
and the heyday of his life been from that date onward to the Great Exhibition of
1851, he would necessarily either have remained himself, on which supposition he
would have been out of tune with the time, and therefore by no possibility popular,
or he would have striven to divest himself of a portion of his own genius, whereby he
would have suffered a serious loss of power, and fallen, as the phrase is, between two
stools. Being impenitently combative, he would have chafed against his time, which
would have disliked his impetuosity, and turned away from his negligent grandeur,
since uncongenial to its own preferences. As it was, he was born and wrote in
the very nick of time, while, during the same period, Wordsworth and Keats, with
temperaments and genius the very opposite of his, had. to wait for recognition till there
supervened a more quietistic and less tumultuous epoch. Byron resembles Vesuvius
in eruption at night, flashing fire through volumes of smoke, while one hears as a
sad soft accompaniment the undertone sobbing of the sea in the Bay below. Hence
his fitfulness, his inequality, his frequent faults of style and expression, hence the
instantaneous magnificence of his best passages. Then the language, as he says of the
sea in the passage Veronica has cited, seems to know its rider. He is incorporated with
it, as he is with the hills when he declares of the mountains, not that he feels them, but
that with him, they " are a feeling." Hence he shares with them their sublimity, but,
likewise, and not infrequently, their ruggedness, their inequality, their repulsiveness.
But, at his very best, he is flawless, without blot or blemish. Is not The Isles of Greece
the finest lyric in the language? I remember, when we were all in Rome together,
being in the Capitoline Museum one day and turning to the pages of the Guide Book
for verification of something about which I was in doubt, and coming on two stanzas
of his, tolerably familiar to one, but which I thereupon read afresh. Pausing at the end
of the first stanza, which was rather slovenly, I said to myself, "So-and-so " (having
in my mind his only successor that has rivalled him in popularity during lifetime)
"would not have been satisfied to have written like that." Then I read on, and, at the
end of the second stanza, felt forced to add, "But he could not have written that"; so
instantaneous, direct, and overpowering was it."

 It is perhaps presumptuous in me," said Lamia modestly, 'to add anything to what
you and Veronica, between you, have been saying. But is not something still wanted to
state the whole truth, something that I suspect was in the mind of both, though neither
has given utterance to it? There is no difficulty in surmising who " So-and-so " is, who
was Byron's successor in contemporaneous popularity, who the delightful poet and
consummate artist to whom you referred. He likewise had the good fortune not to be
born out of his own time, but in it absolutely, and to be all through the meridian of his

poetic activity one with it? A second time as far as poets are concerned, the Hour and the Man met and co-operated. But what a different Hour and what a different Man! Like the thunderstorm described in Vivien as " moaning into other lands," Byron's thunder notes had rolled away; and there were instead, " languid pulses of the oar," " the long gray fields at night," " the glimmering dawn " the lime a summer home of murmurous wings," " bowery hollows crowned with summer sea," " O death in life, the days that are no more," and such passages as

The steer forgot to graze,

And, where the hedge-row cuts the pathway, stood, Leaning his horns into the neighbour field, And lowing to his fellows. From the woods Came voices of the well-contented doves.

Such are the thousand-and-one exquisite touches, the magical lines, the passages brief but all-sufficing, that enchanted a generation, and can never fail to delight lovers of perfect poetic Art. And what was the central and best period of his productivity? It began in 1832, and culminated, in the opinion of most, about thirty years later, a long time for a poet to be at his best; and, with the exception of the miscarriage of the revolutionary attempts of 1848, not to be followed by real new birth till the Commune of 1871, the thirty years after 1832 were years of "peace, retrenchment, and reform," the gradual abolition of abuses, and optimistic horoscopes of the pacific, harmonious, refined Future of Mankind. Hence, in accordance with the theory advanced by Veronica, the Hour helped the Man, and the Man was the artistic mirror of the Hour. Have I," she added, drawing closer to the Poet, been talking nonsense, and only travestying what Veronica and you have been saying? If so, forgive me."

' Dear Lamia," he said, ' I have been listening to you with unqualified approval. You have rounded off our conference, and by exhausting it have brought it to a harmonious conclusion."

I thought to myself that if I ventured to add to the literature of egotism by extolling the Garden that I Love in the same harmonious manner' in which our mutual-admiration-society had been seconding each other's views about poetry, Lamia would have gone round it until she had found some abominable flaw, some flower that had failed, some combination of colour that had only partially succeeded, and made me smart for my self-complacency.

But surely she would find it difficult to discover flaws at this moment. I have never been able to reconcile myself quite to rose-beds pure and simple, with nothing to decorate the interspaces. Accordingly I persuaded the Poet to put, in a newly planted rose-bed that has done, this very first year, excellently well, and will continue to flower during the rest of the year till very severe frost comes, since they are all tea roses, groups of longiflorum lilies, now in all the snowy splendour of their long large bells and healthy green leaves; and the effect is most pleasing. I ought to add that the bed has a wide border of lilac-coloured violas, which take their catalogue name, I believe, from some nurseryman, but which we call Quaker Pet, by reason of their subdued lilac hues. Among the rose-beds there are specio-sum lilies, and in yet others the gorgeous Lilium japonicum. The method can be applied with equal success, indeed perhaps with still more, to beds of certain China roses. With one of these given up to Laurette Messimy, I have, flowering among them, annual marguerite carnations, and the combination has elicited much admiration. Not far from it is another China rose-bed dappled, so to speak, with Salvia farinacea, whose flowers, to the eye of the uninstructed, look for all the world like lavender.

Apropos of lavender, of which Lamia is particularly fond, I have a little story to tell which I will set down here, since the telling of it to some of our garden visitors has seemed to interest them. Several years ago I was at Stratford-on-Avon, then still more or less left to its primitive quiet and unpretentiousness; the house in which Shakespeare is reputed to have been born, looking then much more credibly such than what this age calls improvements have made it look. Yet more surrendered to the kindly nursing of Time and untouched by the tidying, smartening-up tastes of to-day, was Anne Hathaway's cottage at Shotover, which exercised over me a peculiar spell, drawing me back to it afternoon after afternoon. I suppose I was influenced by the feeling that the young Shakespeare had been in its garden many a time and oft, by moonlight, in starlight, at all hours of the day and night, and equally so in the ingle-nook of its cottage hearth. The wrinkled old dame who then lived there believed herself to be, and probably was, a collateral descendant of Anne Hathaway; and she got so accustomed to my daily visits that we became close friends, and used to sit together, with her nut-brown hand in mine, and let our talk ramble backward in a dear, ignorant, semi-imaginative sort of way; and once we had tea together, which pleased her vastly and me no less. She seemed to feel real regret when I told her I was leaving Stratford on the morrow; so, before we parted, she led me into the cottage garden, as rustic as herself, plucked a large bunch of lavender twigs, and, as she gave them to me, said ' If you plant out these in May, They will grow both night and day."

Sure enough, May it was; but, though I was leaving Stratford, I was not going home for some days yet. So I kept the lavender-twigs moist in my sponge-bag; and from these, for the kindly old lady's rhyming saw came true, is descended all the lavender that Lamia loves so. I had the honour for, as you may suppose, such indeed I deemed it of giving some cuttings of it to Tennyson for his garden at Aldworth; and, later on, to the most gifted English actress of our time, who has appeared in every leading female part of humour, majesty, and playfulness in Shakespeare's dramas, to the delectation of us all. Do you wonder if we always call our lavender Anne Hathaway's Lavender '? It is now nearly in full bloom; and I noticed to-day the white butterflies flitting over and among it, almost as thick as fireflies among the ripening corn of a Tuscan podere.

I believe I have said somewhere that among all the princely personages of the garden, the Rose, the Rose is queen. But now, in the very heart of June, I feel that neither I, nor any one, has written of the Rose as it deserves. The Poet is continually admonishing me not to indulge in the prevailing sin of exaggeration and excessive emphasis in style. But what language, what music, could overmuch extol the beauty, the splendour, the homeliness, the pride, the humility, the fragrance,-the independence, the accommodating temper, the clambering, rambling, creeping vagrancy of the Rose? At this moment the world seems one vast rose-garden. Veronica, who sparingly breaks into paeans of enthusiasm, deeming it better, in that terrible conscience of hers, to temper our exuberant admiration with measured eulogies, returns again and again to the beds bordered by the subdued lilac loveliness of Quaker Maid violas, but for the rest dedicated to the roses, from snowy white to dazzling scarlet, got from France last

November, and now in their virgin bloom. But the Poet prefers bushes of Maiden's-Blush, where they keep company with long unfettered trailers of single, double, and semi-double briars, soaring, curving, falling, sweeping the ground, breathing and blooming in their own heedless, Bohemian way. I need scarcely add that where the Poet is, there too is Lamia; and Lamia introduces the feminine note into the colour and perfume of this secluded spot by proclaiming that the Rose and Love are one; at the same time asking him ' Are they not?"

' Yes, Lamia," he answers gallantly, ' Love and the Rose are one; and you are one with both."

Never did I see two such persons for thinking, feeling, and saying the same thing, at the same moment, in the same manner. ' Happy, happy, happy pair!" I am forced to exclaim, in the language of Dryden's Ode in Honour of St. Cecilia s Day. None will deny that Lamia is fair; and assuredly, in respect of his tender affection for her, the Poet is the bravest of the brave. I wish I had half his courage.

But the Rose. Was not that my theme? And here am I, diverted from it by Lamia and her unaccountable attractiveness. What is there the Rose cannot, and will not do? It will cover the Palaces of Kings, and just as gladly embroider the porches of the lowly. It is as happy in the untrimmed hedge as in the well-ordered garden. It can look after itself, and needs no more help than the cloud or the wave. Yet it tolerates interference with no loss of temper, and with its habitual smile. The Rose is queen, but is a countrymaid likewise. It belongs to no class, but is at home with all. Of all love-gifts it is the most expressive and the most seductive. Is not the well-known Rose of Magdeburg one of the most touching incidents in history? What a low fellow, deep down, with the soul of an Italian postilion, was Napoleon, to be so unchivalrous yes, brutally disingenuous, to the lovely Queen of Prussia! Roses welcome our birth, are sponsors at the baptismal font, bridesmaids at our nuptials, mourners and white-robed petitioners to heaven at our interment. They hold their full Court only in summer, but they reign during three of the seasons of the year, and are not always absent from their kingdom during the fourth. And how they vary in character! some being retiringly shy, some self-possessed and dauntless, some attractively modest, while others seem proud of and almost flaunt their beauty. There are roses that seem to think they are the plain ones of the family, and seek to hide themselves and escape attention. But, as Veronica remarked yesterday, the nearer that garden roses approximate to the wild eglantine, the more they charm. Some of the new Ramblers Blush Rambler, for instance make you stop and look at them just as children do. But I must not excite jealousy among them by naming some and being silent about others. Besides, have you not remarked there are roses that, like human beings, look their best at one age, their least well at another? The handsome youth sometimes expands into a man you do not turn to look at, and another, unnoticeable in the meridian of his life, becomes picturesque-looking in his decline. It is the same with Roses; save that, like women, they are never altogether plain at any age, if one lingers on their looks, and only has eyes wherewith to see.

Lamia, who has read the foregoing, and says nothing in contradiction of it, and who has access to all the Poet's MSS., shows me the following Sonnet as in some degree bearing on the above theme, and says that perhaps it will, for some readers, render my fresh instalment of ' horticultural literature' more tolerable. So, obedient to her wishes, I append it. I ask her when she thinks it was written, and she answers characteristically, but perhaps not untruly, Probably some ten or fifteen years hence."

In this resplendent Autumn of your days You seem yet lovelier even than in Spring, More musical in voice, more young in gaze, More dear, more richly dowered in everything. Now in your promise lurks no veering vow, Nor in your tearful tenderness caprice; Blossom and fruit together deck you now, And Love abides, companioned by Peace. O keep then as you are, nor let Time cast One shadow on the dial of your days, Nor wintry rime nor desolating blast That beauty rob where nothing yet decays. But should that last petition be denied, You still will find me, reverent, at your side.

One would naturally expect peace to reign uninterrupted in a Garden, if anywhere. The very word suggests tranquillity, retirement, aloofness from contending passion, even from conflicting emotions, and, above all, from the heats of controversy, and, doubtless, what the name suggests, the garden itself corresponds with, to the casual unconcerned visitor, who, coming to it from the paving-stones of Pall Mall, or the ballroom floors of Mayfair, exclaims, There!" seats himself among its invisible perfumes, lets his eye wander over its rainbow colours, or saunters among its summer roses or its autumnal lilies. But, be yourself the owner, nay more, the conceiver and guardian of the Garden, you will indeed be the favoured of Heaven, with not even the ' critic on the hearth' to dispute your sway, if the demon of disagreement do not find his way into your earthly paradise. Indeed, if you be a person of many minds and many moods, varying winds of doctrine will from time to time disturb your peace, and rival theories of horticulture, as of writing, will invade your serenity.

' How very irregular," says Veronica, ' the things in this bed are looking!"

'I did not want them," I reply, 'to be quite regular, but they will be regular enough when they have all attained their full growth."

' And pray," strikes in Lamia, ' pray, when will that be? I observe that the Golden Year is always coming, but never comes. Will it arrive just as the early October frosts wither all your posies? At present I see the grossest irregularities in this supposed respectable enclosure. Not that, personally, I have the slightest objection to irregularity, for I am not going to cast stones from my own glass-house; but, as you sometimes say, let us look facts frankly in the face, and manfully of course, manfully confess that this is at present a rag-bag of a bed, with no apparent design in it, and luxuriating in conspicuous disorder."

The Poet smiles, and, as usual, strives to make us all ' harmonious' once more.

Are you not," he says, returning to the point we discussed a short time ago in regard to Poetry? In gardens, as in literature, there may be too solicitous finish, or too much carelessness; and in an age that inclines perhaps overmuch to the former in verse, one may reasonably expect to find the same bias in gardening. Should we not have a care lest, in both cases, craft should take the place of true Art? '

And this garden?" says Lamia, stealing close to him, and with voice, smile, and intonation, leaving him, or any one for that matter, no choice but to reply assentingly: What, in literature, does the garden that we love resemble?"

Would it be, Lamia, think you, As You Like It r

She clapped her hands. ' O, yes; and you shall be the Duke, if I may be ' She paused, as if suddenly embarrassed.

What you are," said the Poet, exchanging sweet words with her, as usual, ' a compound of Rosalind and Celia."

Am I to be nothing in this literary fantasy of a garden?" I pleaded.

' You!" exclaimed Lamia. Obviously, you are Jaques, moralising and " full of matter "; or perhaps the well-known " fool i' the forest." '

And Veronica?"

' Veronica is the intelligent audience, dealing out justice to us, " merely players," yet at the same time reminding me of a line traditionally attributed to the author of As Tou Like It, though not to be found in any of his works:

We are all both actors and spectators too."

'And attributed to him," said the Poet, 'I doubt not, correctly; for he, more than any other man that ever lived, is master of apt, illustrative expression, by which we recognise him at once."

Thus we fleet away the time, in the garden that we love, contributing nothing to the excitement, but, I am generously assured, occasionally to the delectation of the time, and feeling that this life of ours, exempt from public haunt, is more sweet than that of painted pomp, and quite as profitable to ourselves and others as more elaborate modes of existence.

Michaelmas. Need I deny it?" said the Poet.

The impeachment was not a very serious one; for Veronica had only been saying that there were days when he seemed utterly incapable of sitting still, though supposed to be at what is ambiguously called work. It hardly can be necessary to say that the morning-room, in which we usually forgather of an evening, and which, described when I told of the modest addition to our home, has proved such an adornment to it, has been allotted to the Poet, for whom Veronica, more flattering in deeds than words, apparently thinks nothing too good. It is enlivened by the morning sun, and one has only to open the door and traverse a short passage, to find oneself in the Garden, on a flower-crowned brick path, up and down which one may pace or meditate with undisturbed will. But, as Veronica had been saying, there are days when this convenient if limited territory does not satisfy him, but he is out and about in an erratic and unaccountable manner.

Need I deny it?" he pleaded. ' There is no inevitable connection between the goodness or badness of work, and the pains or pleasure a man takes in doing it. The aphorism c Genius is patience," was originally coined by Buffon, and not by any of the various persons to whom, in these inaccurate days, it is from time to time ascribed; and Buffon was dozing somewhat, I think, when he said it. Would it not be nearer the truth, but still not the whole truth, to say that Genius is a mixture of impatience and patience? But all the impatience and patience in the world will not produce works of Genius, if the workers be not themselves endowed at birth with that sovran gift. Most of us are wanting in patience, and at times have impatience enough to subdue all difficulties, if that quality had in itself any such power, which, alas, it has not. One keeps bursting into the Garden, as you say, because there are moments when one cannot sit still. As long as one has freedom to move, and is seized of an idea, one feels as though one had dominion over all the kingdoms of earth and air, and no resistance was offered to utterance and imagination uncontrolled. One sits down and suddenly one finds oneself the mere satrap of a narrow and recalcitrant province. If impelled to write musically one would fall a-mumbling were one to be at rest, and subside into the dreariest prose. The result in one's own case may be but indifferent; but such is the operation. Do the judges absolve me?"

' You leave the Court," said Veronica, with no stain on your character; and, so long as you don't break one of my Chippendale chairs, or upset and chip one of my old flower-glasses, you may stampede, my dear, at your end of the house as often and long as you like."

' But," added Lamia for Veronica had left us to look after our creature comforts elsewhere the Court thinks it only right to assign you some little compensation for the stigma under which you have been lying. It is only by some such process as you have described that any work of art, whether in literature, painting, or music, is imbued with true charm."

' Probably," he replied. ' Only remember what I said, that it does not necessarily impart it to them."

' But tell me," said Lamia, ' is it easy, indeed is it possible, to say unerringly if a work possesses true charm?"

' Apparently not," he answered; for though there is such a thing as real charm, there is such another as pseudo-charm; in a word, the original and a copy; and I observe that copies impose themselves upon a good many supposed experts. A few years ago there was a lively controversy in art circles whether a certain picture, bequeathed by Signor Morelli to Madame Minghetti, widow of the one-time Italian Prime Minister, and alleged to be by Leonardo da Vinci, was an original picture by that supreme painter, a copy, or the work of some other hand. Most experts maintained it was the first; and, as one of these happened to be a friend of my own, I asked for his opinion, since doubts, by no means ill supported, were thrown on its genuineness. He replied that he would pledge his professional reputation as to its being a genuine Leonardo. "As you know," he said, " the picture has gone to America; but I have a large and admirable photograph of it, which I will show you." He drew this from a portfolio, and placed it on his easel. Instantaneously I said to myself, "That is not by Leonardo," but I was not so presumptuous as to utter that conclusion aloud.

Very shortly, a man came forward and said, " painted that picture," and proved the truth of his assertion beyond power of contradiction. I am no expert in the judging of pictures, or probably I should have been just as much mistaken as my experienced and accomplished friend. The actual painter was a consummate master of technical craft, and, after reading the theory propounded by my friend and others, that the surest way to test the genuineness of a picture is to observe some inevitable detail, such as the contour of the ears or the size and shape of the finger-nails, and having most carefully studied the workmanship and, if one may say so, the unconscious tricks of Leonardo, he had reproduced these with the utmost accuracy. A thoroughly expert draughtsman and colourist, he had thus imposed on other experts, but not on those ignorant of technique in painting, yet loving pictures and not insensible to their charm, and what the Italians call the non so che that constitutes charm. This is rather a long disquisition, Lamia, but you provoked it."

And I am glad I did, and I want you to answer yet another question. Can similar mistakes be made concerning books, and charm in them?"

' Undoubtedly," he replied; ' and, in so far as one may trust one's own judgment, they are being constantly made by the professed experts, and for the same reason. It is not often that they fail to perceive charm when it is really there; but they ever and again ascribe it to pages whose writers, exceedingly clever persons, have more or less caught the trick, as the phrase is, of the real charmers."

But how," asked Lamia, ' is one to discriminate between the two?"

' One cannot, so far as demonstration and the convincing of others is concerned; for, if they do not of themselves perceive the difference, there is no way of communicating it to them. One can do it only for oneself. To feel real charm and distinguish it from deliberate imitation, depends on the power of instinctive appreciation. It is one of those intuitions that cannot be argued about."

Has real charm," I asked, ' some one quality or characteristic by which we may recognise its presence or its absence?"

'I think so," he replied. 'The quality is unconsciousness, and charm appertains to the essence of the person or thing endowed with it. It cannot be acquired, it cannot be got rid of, and its results are produced without effort, since the person who has it cannot help producing them."

But surely," I said, ' there must be effort in the production of every work of art, whether it be a poem, a picture, or a symphony."

Unquestionably; but the charm in it is not produced by effort. Intention, technique, craft, must contribute to the production of such works; but that which makes them charming, if they are so, is something quite apart from these. Pope, for instance, is a great writer, and a considerable poet, and abounds in intention, craft, and technique; but he rarely, if ever, has charm. He did not have it in himself, and therefore could not radiate it. Spenser is a supreme instance of charm as a poet. Apparently, he could not help being charming, save where the theme forbade the exhibition of it; and even this is very rare with him. Mozart is a supreme instance of it in music; and I should be disposed to say Raphael is in painting."

Both Lamia and I seemed to be in an unusually argumentative mood, and went on, pressing the Poet very hard.

' I know," said Lamia, ' it is approaching rank blasphemy to ask the question I am going to put.

But has the Garden that we love no real charm? It certainly has been produced with no little effort."

' I think, Lamia, I can elude, while answering you. For me, at least, the Garden that we love does possess charm, but not arising from anything we have done to it. Save for its native position and accidents, which we did not create, it would not be charming, though it might still be beautiful. The magnificent timber that is not in it but near it, the park in front of it, the park behind it, the architecture of the old Manor House, the majestic guardianship of the secular oak, its facing southeast these, and other conditions we did not create, render it charming; and, if I may say so, it is yet more charming when you are in it."

I confess I began to think there must be something sophistical, not to say unsound, in the argument, when there was resorted to something very like bribery and corruption to enforce it. But that suspicion, perhaps naturally, did not strike Lamia, who observed ' I allow," she said, I rarely make an effort, but I know a good many people who never do so, yet are very much the reverse of charming. But, though I too feel the charm of the Garden that we'love, I certainly am not aware of adding to it."

If you were said the Poet, taking advantage of her inadvertence, ' you would cease to be charming. Women," he went on, ' are more frequently charming than men, because they are less self-conscious. Look at flowers, also. There is not a rose in all the garden, however beautiful, delicate, wonderfully complex, it may be, that is as charming as the wild-rose in the hedge-row. Is not the truth this, that the word charm is used too indiscriminately, and indeed, by some people, at every turn, and of everything? Moreover, in poetry at least, it is a quality that of late years has come to be over-estimated, relatively to other qualities. There is often a certain effeminate sensuousness in charm, that is very attractive to the present generation, which overlooks other elements in art of equal, probably of yet greater, importance. The Earthly Paradise is more charming, in the proper sense of the word, than Paradise Lost. Yet will any one say it is as great? Does it not, in comparison, on the score of greatness, sink into insignificance? So you see, Lamia, one tries to keep the balance even. As I have granted, women are more charming than men; but I will venture to add, men, that is to say some men, are greater than any women."

Womanly women," said Lamia, ' will gladly accord to man superiority in that respect, so they be left superior in the other. I would sooner be a wild-rose than win battles or electrify Senates. All the same one is glad there are human beings who can electrify Senates and win battles, and we should sorely miss them if they did not exist."

' The distinction," said the Poet, ' seems to me a true and universal one. Nor does one see sufficient reason, despite the protests of an active but small minority, to suppose that it will not be a permanent one. Look at most women, when their faces are in repose. What are they doing? They are dreaming. Look at men. They are thinking."

' Unless," observed Lamia, ' the men happen to be poets. Then they are doing both."

Q. E. D.," I murmured sardonically, under my breath.

The foregoing conversation had not been wholly uninteresting to me. But when it ended in the usual battledore and shuttlecock game of reciprocated sweetnesses, I wandered round the garden for neutral company, and fell to wondering whether it is more attractive in late spring or in the early days of autumn. I saw it affirmed in print the other day that the writers who say a beautiful flower-garden can be had for eight, and sometimes for nine, months in the year, are misleading people. I can only reply that the person who made that statement has but an imperfect acquaintance with gardening and its possibilities. Should there come a heavy and continuous fall of snow at the beginning of March, and should it lie for the whole of that month, then

I grant the ordinary course of nature has been for once interrupted. But when, in the south or west of England, does that happen? I have known something like it, but only something like it, occur just once in a now pretty long experience. For the rest, I am prepared not only to do battle for the ' eight or nine months ' period, but to go still farther, and to plead that no month in the year is out of doors wholly flowerless, at least, in the south, south-east, south-west, and west of England. I speak only of what I know, and what the Garden That I Love has taught me. New Year's Day, let us say, has come and gone, and January is moving slowly on. Choose but the aspect aright, and prepare the soil with due knowledge, and what is there to prevent the winter-aconites from greeting the New Year, and accompanying it till

January be spent? Do not suppose this will infallibly happen the very first January after you put the bulbs into the ground, though even then it may. You must not, however, count on it. But the year after that, and for every succeeding January, the winter-aconites will illuminate with their golden cressets the spot where you have placed them. We have two little nooks for them immediately on either side of the entrance-door that looks south-east, and they never fail to come forth and show themselves in the very first month of the year, signalling to their brethren in the turf under the old oak to be up and about, and not long laggard after these early risers. The most effective clump of them, no doubt, is in a small round open bed under a tulip-tree, as yet of moderate dimensions, though it has already begun to flower in the late summer. But these winter aconites open a little later, by reason of the partial shade above them given by the pretty thick branches of the tulip-tree, even when still bare of leaves. That little round space serves a double purpose; for, while the winter-aconites in full flower there cover the whole of it, below them and out of sight are colchicum bulbs, which the ignorant call winter-crocuses, given me many years ago by the wife of a famous Field-Marshal and a woman of exquisite taste. They are of the pale lavender colour, much more rare and difficult to get than the larger, deep-coloured ones, which we also have; and when their foliage fades, and can be carefully cut or pulled away, up come, to replace them, the strong, vigorous leaves of the Colchicum. But only the leaves; which in summer themselves wax wilted and fade, and then leafless flowers of the most delicate colour and dainty beauty come up, and look like Fairyland under the then lavishly furnished tulip-tree. And does the horticultural sceptic I refer to suppose it is impossible to coax yellow crocuses for the yellow ones are the hardiest to face the perils of the early days of the year, or to get snowdrops to do the same, without any coaxing at all? And the primrose? I do not speak of garden primulas, but of the wild and simple native of the woodlands. Is it beneath one's notice, and undeserving of a place in the garden? In the one we love there is always a place allotted to it, and more than one place; and it must be a very peculiar January, one deep in snow, or hard frost-bound, for a certain number of these unaffected flowers not to be awake and up somewhere then. I will not engage that on your rockery you shall have Cyclamen coum in bloom, but you may, and with it the small, modest, but clustering and effective flowers of the Potentilla.

But, like a prudent general, I keep my best and bravest battalion for the final charge; and I ask this sceptic of gardens whether he has ever seen the Iris stylosa? I saw them first in a but-little-cared-for garden at Bordighera pretty long ago, and I stood wondering under the spell of enchantment. I brought some home with me, or, rather, had them sent to me late in the spring when they had finished flowering, and for the first two years made a deplorable misuse of them. They showed ample leafage, but did not flower; and then it struck me that they had not been accustomed to high living, and I had been overfeeding them, and the muzzle must be put on by giving them the leanest of fare. In plain words, the soil was much too rich for them. I took them up, broke them into small pieces, and planted them in a sheltered yet sunny position, and in a mass of rubble mixed with light poor soil. Since then they have produced an uninterrupted succession of flowers from the beginning of December till the coming of the first swallow. Veronica delights in them, and some are always taken to her boudoir, where freesias also are welcome, but from which flowers of strong perfume are rigidly excluded.

But this is not winter, whose contribution to the ' nine months in the year' I think I have established; nor yet spring, whose floral reputation needs no defending, for no one would dream of assailing it. We are, at the time at which I wrote, at the parting of the ways between a prodigious summer and an equally splendid but less ostentatious autumn; or, to put it differently, October is protecting the rear of departing summer. I cannot help a little self-complacency just now, since the garden has this year had a conspicuous triumph. The unbroken drought of July and August had dealt irreparable desolation in every other garden I have seen or heard of; and the ruin was completed by the hurricane of wind that accompanied the advent of showers, even then not too bountiful. Never before has the Garden That I Love been in greater beauty. There is a vacuum, a failure, nowhere; and even Veronica is unreserved in her admiration. She was away during August, and returned only in the early days of September. I had abstained from all report of its condition, and my silence led her to conclude, not that no news was good news, but very bad news indeed. In order to keep up the comedy, I arranged that on her return she should enter from the lane, in order that what there was to show should burst upon her nearly all at once.

I suppose," she said, ' the Garden is a wreck, like all that I have seen elsewhere."

It has been a sadly trying time," I replied evasively.

In another moment we emerged from the plantation near the well, and suddenly the Garden was in sight. She stopped full short, as the phrase is, held up both hands, and exclaimed 'Oh!"

That was all, but how much it was, and one was more than rewarded for all one had done to baffle the long-continued drought. Let me say once more that due digging and manuring in May ought to furnish a garden with protection against Fate in any ordinary year. But I had misgivings that this was going to be an extraordinary one; and as, two winters ago, we made, under the old Manor Pound, a good large tank to receive the rain-water from all the guttering round the old red-roofed farm buildings still remaining near the house, including those of the house itself, there was an ample supply at the beginning of June. Not to everything, but only to beds and borders stocked with things planted in them at the end of May, we began at once applying rain-water after the sun had gone off them. Many persons will assert that watering does no good, and sometimes does serious hurt. But that depends on the nature of the water. If the water be hard, or, indeed, other than bona-fide rain-water, that would be so; for, of course, watering has a tendency to bring roots and rootlets to the surface in expectation of what they like so much; and the process, once started, must be persisted in, Persist we did; and we followed up the watering with periodical hoeing. By the end of the month everything looked wonderfully forward, and then the nine weeks' drought began. Confident in the resources of the tank, we continued our evening labours with excellent effect. But, by the middle of August, the gardener said the tank was very low. In a few more days it was empty, and the drought and sun-heat were more pitiless than ever. In our resolve not to be beaten there was no slackening; and though our modest resources can produce only hand water-barrels, these were trundled down to the river and back for three or four hours every day. I felt, however, that, though no complaint had been uttered, the grind' was too much in such weather, and so reverted to another device. There is another tank, which Cowper, perhaps, who introduces into his verse such a realistic line as ' The stable yields a stercoraceous heap," would have described more minutely, but of which I will content myself with saying that it yielded some three to four hundred gallons a day of soft, but not quite so savoury, a liquid. Needs must when ' the devil of a drought' drives; and, as Veronica and Lamia were absent, it did not much matter.

After three days, clouds began to muster on the horizon; rumblings were heard in the distance, and, finally, down came the rain. The situation, as they say, had been saved. But that represents very inadequately what had happened. Coming on the top you see, I cannot help adopting the language of the grateful and triumphant gardener and his help of the use of the unsavoury tank, the rain put the finishing touch to our efforts, and produced the effect that caused Veronica to halt in astonishment, and exclaim 'Oh!"

One of the results has been that everything is prodigiously tall. The dahlias are nine, the sunflowers thirteen, feet high, even Montbretia close on four, and Salvia farinacea, which most persons take for tall lavender, fully five feet high. Other things, herbaceous, biennial, and annual, have shot upward in like proportion. But, just as the moralising Watts said, ' The mind's the measure of the man," so the flowering of plants is the final standard of their worth and loveliness; and they are all not only divinely tall, but most divinely efflorescent. I could not resist feeling, as I walked round them to-day, that beds, and borders, and groups, had projected a private flower-show of their own, and are now ' showing' against each other. Were I the prize-giver, I should be perplexed to know to which to assign it. Poet's Corner another, if you remember, of Veronica's christenings is a garden in itself. The variegated maize, the daturas, and the dark castor-oil plant, seem to have entered into an almost fraudulent conspiracy to deceive the unwary, the white bells of the datura appearing to belong to all three, so cunningly have they mingled with each other. Yet, if I were compelled to come to a decision, I almost think that I should assign the gold medal to the oval bed seen through the leafy branches of the Hungarian lime, which is at once simple and imposing. So simple is it, that its composition is soon told. In the centre are tall tropical-looking cannas, and round them variegated maize, bronze castor-oil, and the dwarfer dark-leafed cannas. Outside these, again, is Montbretia in splendid flower, and an edging of China-aster sinensis. Yet when I wander off in another direction, and come upon the Lobelia cardinalis, the Calceolaria ampkxicaulis, and the fibrous-rooted begonias, in chromatic combination, I feel that I have been unjust, after all, and that here the first prize should have been adjudged.

How much longer will it last? Like the poppies, of whom it has been written

They flaunt like glory, and fade as fast, so over all this loveliness stretches the lengthening shadow of the declining year; and I could not but repeat to myself the stanza

She wore the silent plaintive grace Of autumn just before its close,

And, on her fair but fading face, The pathos of November rose.

We were sitting in the lime parlour, the name given to it by Veronica, who much affects the spot, roofed by the leafy dome of the weeping Hungarian lime, which every other year needs to have its ever-encroaching territory recognised and marked out afresh by unbarked timber pillars or supports. What led up to the following conversation I quite forget; but it began by the Poet observing 'In no community is literature so little reverenced, and are men-of-letters so little regarded, as in England. I am by no means sure this is a disadvantage to the latter; indeed, I am disposed, on the whole, to think it is for their good. But the fact is certain, and to the nation at large it can hardly fail to be injurious."

What is the cause? ' asked Lamia.

Is it not the practical character of our race? ' I suggested. ' Our countrymen are moved to admiration only by actual, patent, and resounding success; but the best literature is not resounding, and the most. self-respecting men-of-letters, as a rule, lead retired lives."

But how about English women? ' asked Veronica.

I am afraid," answered the Poet, that as regards women also, the phenomenon holds equally good. Privately, and in their hearts, I daresay they have a warm admiration for superior talent of every kind, and a still warmer for real genius. But probably men cherish the same sentiment privately. In France, in Italy, even in Germany, though perhaps at present in a waning degree, admiration is openly and enthusiastically expressed."

Is what you have said asked Lamia, ' equally true of painting and music in this country? ' ' Not to the same extent, by any means; and for the reason I have already suggested. Painters exhibit their pictures, and the compositions of musicians are heard and heard frequently; so that both may have that practical and patent success I spoke of. Moreover, since painters can paint the portraits of kings, princes, and other eminent persons, and thus minister to the sense of self-importance, rich men can buy, and so glorify themselves by the purchase and monopoly of the pictures, and practical and patent success is thus achieved. But I still doubt whether their patrons have a genuine reverence for them. They regard them rather as a flattering form of usefulness."

' Has the example," said Veronica, ' thus set in the highest quarters, anything to do with the absence of reverence on the part of the nation generally?"

' I rather think so. We are an aristocratic, I use the word in its conventional, not in its proper sense, some would say a snobbish people, and so imitate our so-called betters, who, in many respects, are often our inferiors."

But may we go back," said Lamia, to the woman's share in the question? I think some of us have a profound reverence, which we scarcely conceal, for superior mental gifts."

If by " some of us," ' said the Poet, smiling, you mean, dear, yourself, it is perfectly true. I am well aware that, if you were allowed, you would go careering through the land on a motor-car, disfiguring the road with leaflets on the unequalled claims to universal admiration and reverence of certain obscure persons. But I do not think your journey would be a very successful one; certainly not as much so as if you distributed leaflets on a new soap or a novel form of underclothing; and, in all probability, you would end by being summoned for forgetting, in your mistaken enthusiasm, the number of miles an hour at which one is by law permitted to raise dust anything rather than Olympian. To be allowed to do that, you must drive a motor-car in rivalry with other motor-cars, in order to have the practical and patent success of placing them on the market, and making them appear to have the largest and longest circulation in the world."

Alas!" said Lamia, with a profound sigh, ' it is so. What is one to do?"

' Nothing," he replied, quite cheerfully. But there are many things worth noting, for which there is no remedy. Indeed, the enduring evils, rather than the passing ones, it is, that are the most interesting."

Is he not provoking," said Veronica, with his philosophic indifference, or, still worse, his amused resignation to what is both mischievous and unfair?"

' Quite incorrigible," said Lamia. ' But I should like to add to what has been said, that, whereas in France and Germany men of genius have almost always had their Egerias, who did not console and encourage them surreptitiously at midnight, but aided and abetted them in the full glare of day, and have survived in story to share their fame, in England the poor Numas endowed by Heaven with superior gifts have rarely had such companions, or, if they had them, consoler and consoled alike have taken pains to hide, both in their life and afterward, any such disgraceful circumstance."

Is it," I asked, because, as I heard a Hungarian lady assert the other day, ' that, in respect of the relations of the sexes, Englishmen, though not all of them, are the only gentlemen in Europe?"

' I suspect," the Poet replied, ' there is some truth in that. Frenchmen openly boast of what an Englishman would feel bound to treat as strictly private and confidential; and French and German ladies have paraded and published stories of feminine generosity which an Englishwoman would have buried in her heart. When Merimee published his Lettres a une Inconnue French people asked, why this anonymity? The mystery was explained by the circumstance that the Inconnue was an Englishwoman. I was reading the other day an article in the leading French Review on the letters written to and by Frau Wesendonk, and the writer fell into raptures over the story they disclosed. For the lady I could not repress my sympathy, pity, and admiration; but I was inspired with deep dislike for everything in Wagner except his genius. The " long disease, my life " of Pope was alleviated by the kindness of two old maids, but treated very differently by Lady Mary Wortley Montagu when Pope would fain have played the part of Abelard to Eloisa; and the infirmities of Cowper were mitigated by the tender domestic attention of Lady Austen and Mrs. Unwin. But Chaucer, but Spenser, but

Shakespeare, but Milton, but Dryden who was their Egeria, if they had one, or who were the sensitive, unselfish beings that stimulated their genius, and softened their sorrows? We can hardly believe they were without such. Modern biographers have striven to discover that secret; for, in these days, as another poet concerning whom no such association has been disclosed, has said, " the many-headed beast must know." But they have groped and ferreted in vain; and, despite Shakespeare's sonnets, " the dark woman" is still shrouded in darkness, his youthful courtship has only furnished doubts as to who really was his wife, and the gropers have not been able to make anything out of the bequest of his bedstead to his widow beyond the fact that his bedstead it was, and that it was left to her."

'But we have changed all that," I observed, in these admirably progressive days; and the loves of Byron, Burns, Shelley, and Keats, have become the property of the whole world."

' That is so," said the Poet; ' but it has scarcely been to their serious advantage; and even they were mild offenders, compared with, say, Chateaubriand, who, not content with pluming himself in his lifetime on what the French nation characteristically call bonnes fortunes, must needs publish posthumous memoirs, to perpetuate his role of conquering hero. As in his case, if in a minor degree, such questionable notoriety for details of incidents of private life have obtained a wider vogue for the writings of the English poets I have just mentioned. But they scarcely needed this vulgar form of advertisement, and they certainly do not stand higher in the esteem of their countrymen in consequence."

' But," said Lamia pleadingly, ' you do not, do you, condemn the French women of intellectual distinction of the eighteenth century, whose names are permanently associated with men to whose mental development their sympathy and encouragement seem to have acted as a stimulus and an encouragement?"

' Far from it, Lamia. But, in the cases to which you refer intellectual sympathy occupies the foreground, and was, and will remain, an honour to both. In this respect, the biographies and diaries of English men-of-letters and their feminine auxiliaries are much behindhand; but, whether because there was little or nothing of the kind to tell, or of the incurable shyness and reserve of the English nature, who shall say? We are the only people in the world who strive to seem more stupid and less interesting than we really are."

' I was wanting," said Lamia, to arrive at that conclusion. If a man deviates in ever so slight a degree from reserve, he runs the risk of being regarded as an egotist. If he deviates from it still more he is looked upon as a " bounder."

' And quite right too," said Veronica. Men ought to be able to fight their own battles, shape their own career, and achieve their purpose, without sympathy. If they fail, then I daresay there will always be a little womanly consolation in reserve for them somewhere."

But how about the sympathetic assistance given by men to intellectual women?" asked Lamia.

Is not that easily answered?" said the Poet. ' Women are interested in men, men are interested in themselves."

How serious we all are to-day!" said Lamia, and I feel the fault is mine. Let me try to repair it by reading to you the following lines I found lying about, and that might have been written in prophetic anticipation of what we have been saying."

We all ' struck the proper attitude' to hear the verses to which Lamia's voice seemed to give at least a quiet movement of melody.

A WOMAN'S AVOWAL

Let others, be there such, aspire

To a resounding life, Leaving unfed the household fire

For heat of public strife, I am content, to choose though free, In no such paths to roam, And only unheard helpmate be

To him who guards my home.

But I can nerve him for the fray

When duty needs his arm, Cheering him onward day by day

With love's attendant charm. And when he may contend no more,

After long strenuous years, I may his waning strength restore

With tenderness and tears.

His closing days will walk with mine

Down age's gentle slope, The shadow of that dear decline

Brightened by lengthening hope.

And should he hence the first depart,

As, for his sake, I crave, I shall embalm him in my heart,

And sanctify his grave.

I half feared her voice, which audibly trembled, would not serve her to the end. But it held out bravely, though through its silvery tone there seemed to sound the minor of suppressed tears. The Poet stroked her hand; Veronica put her arm round her; and thus I left them, strange happy trinity, to meditate once more in the unpolemical beauty of the Garden That I Love.

February 28. They are out! They're all out!"

'What? Which? Where?"

It was Lamia who had come running in, to announce the above somewhat vague tidings; and, among us, we fired off those more precise inquiries.

Why, the bees, of course, and, with them, two sulphur butterflies."

Sure enough, out they were for the first time this year, making such music as never was, on the only instruments as yet accessible, to their delicate touch. It has been a long, lingering winter, and, though it is the last day of February, one has to go hunting in the warmest and most sheltered nooks, to discern here and there a few short-stalked primroses. But the wind has veered to the sanguine south; the sun has routed every cloud from the sky; and the winter-aconites, hitherto offering only button-shaped buds to the view, have opened wide their eyes; and it is among them that the bees, announced by Lamia, are so busily buzzing. Need I say that we all sallied out to behold this first indication, and hear the first notes, of adumbrated Spring?

We are not bee-keepers, for the bees keep themselves, and have a vast establishment deep under the rafters of one of the farm-yard sheds, which were fully described when first eheu fugaces I I see it was thirteen years ago one began to coo like a self-complacent cushat, as Lamia puts it, over the garden that I love. Veronica occasionally betrays her housekeeping propensities by asking if we male creatures are not going to do something towards bringing in a portion at least of the honey there must lurk in the invisible home of the industrious community. But we give her no encouragement, and again plead that this is Liberty Hall, where even bees are to be allowed to work undisturbed, at their own sweet will.

They are repaying us now," says Lamia, ' for our forbearance. Listen to them as they gather the pollen."

A lingering Winter and a tardy Spring are what we always should like in this part of the world. Last year the weather made quite different arrangements, and the consequence was that plums, pears, and even apples fell helpless victims to the topsy-turvydom of nature and the seasons. Now the promise of the three, so far as one yet can judge, is magnificent, and one already, in fancy, sees purple clusters of early prolific plums thicker than leaves on south wall branches, and Lamia declares she can already taste the sharp sub-flavour of the ' councillors of the court," and the luscious sweetness of the ever-popular ' good Christians."

' You will know more about that," says warier Veronica, ' when the young May moon has ceased shining. Meanwhile, cloy your appetite with bare imagination of a feast."

March 12. Twelve days have now passed since the foregoing hopeful tidings were announced; and since then the season has moved on apace without check or hindrance. One can see that everything is astir underground, and many things spreading themselves out above it. The wizard sun has changed the look of the world, especially in the garden, and most of all under that oak which has seen Celt, Roman, Saxon, Norman, and our hybridised selves occupy the English land. The same tale can be told of the crocus, and even of the snowdrop, as of the primroses. They have lagged in an unprecedented manner. But the golden colonies under the oak are now all ablaze, our wealth being, as Lamia reminds me the Poet has somewhere said, ' not under, but above, the ground." The white, purple, and lilac ones are slower a'coming; but here and there they are following suit, and in a day or two will overtake their yellow comrades. By the middle of the month, as we all know for even in this desultory, superficial, tit-bit age, almost everybody knows one or two brief quotations from Shakespeare the daffodils ought to be taking the winds of March with beauty'; but this year they are behindhand in their wooing. It is just as well, for it gives the more modest, if many-coloured, crocuses a fair chance of being appreciated. Nature never intended the two to come together. I wish so many people, and among them those who have the ordering of royal and public gardens, would not plant crocuses in so formal and regular a manner, but imitate the admirable irregularity of the heavens in the ordering and disposition of the stars. I am sure, if you saw them, you would think the crocus patches under the oak have come there of themselves, they have such a haphazard appearance. In beds and borders, I grant you, you may without any reproach, from me at least, plant your crocuses in long uninterrupted lines; for beds and borders perforce betray the hand and co-operation of man; and until they are one mass of growth and colour in August and September, and the ground is entirely hidden, it is no good pretending that chance has been your gardener. That is why early Spring is the season for wild gardening. The change from grey to green turf, dappled with daisies after the long sluggish months of winter, suggests the spontaneous lavishness of nature; and illusion, that happiest and most beneficent of all things, is thus produced and prolonged during the burgeoning season.

But Spring is not here yet, so it is no use pretending that it is, though Lamia and the Poet, ever ready to be illusioned by agreeable omens, and always ready to build on them airy structures, compared with which castles in Spain are solid edifices, persuade themselves, and vainly try to persuade Veronica and me, that it is.

' You have neither insight nor foresight," Lamia says to me. You sometimes assert, in doubtful compliment to me, that I have some of Spring's characteristics, of course the most objectionable ones, uncertainty and capriciousness, and that I occasionally resemble it. Let us suppose it is true, and it follows as the day the night what an irrelevant collocation of cause and consequence in our all-wise, but, perhaps because, unscientific, Stratford Common Councillor! that I must know more about Spring than you do, or, be it reverently said, even Veronica does; and whatever I know, the Poet knows, only better. Therefore, it is Spring. Listen to the thrushes, unless you have ears and hear not! They are a little behindhand in beginning their duets, sonatas, and symphonies on their Spring instruments, though March has been drumming in the trees and up the chimney; but they are audibly tuning up now, adagio adagio, andante, and rondo con moto espressivo, will soon follow."

' Yes," I said, even I have observed that the first indications of love-making by them have begun."

Do you mean to hint that I am like them in that also? On the contrary, I am trying to take a lesson from them in that respect; being so ignorant of that popular accomplishment. But, rather to my perplexity, I observe that, with them, the preliminaries of the Ars Amandi I must ask the Poet, some time when Veronica is not present, if Ovid mentions it in that classical work, Dryden's translation of which I am not allowed so much as to look at, poor little innocent! strongly resemble the strategy and tactics of war. Look at them now. All the blackbirds say as yet is " Come on!" and they fight and flutter at each other from dawn to dark."

' Only the males," I suggest; the females are hanging about, and looking on, though seemingly with much impartial sympathy."

' Exactly," says Lamia; ' but therein lies my interest, and my desire to be instructed by them. That the eager females, like the tender-hearted matrons egging on the gladiators in the Roman amphitheatre to maul each other, are the instigators of the feathered fight, I cannot doubt, but I want to find out how they do it, so that I may follow suit. Love and war, arma virumque cano, these are the eternal enduring twin; so that, manlike, you can be sentimental and pugnacious at one and the same time, and we interested but amused observers of your antics when what you are pleased to call the season of love and love-making sets in."

I never said so," I pleaded; I leave that to the Poets."

You had better leave everything to them," she replied, ' for they know more about everything than you, with your practical common-sense views, are ever likely to know about anything. But, before we quit the subject of the Ars Amatoria let me remind you of what a poet, pretty well versed in male ways of love-making, says, and it is no use your protesting against it, for nobody will believe you.

The bird that sings within the brake, The swan that swims upon the lake, One mate, and one alone, will take, While Man

Just look at those two thrushes! Like the two armies in the "Battle of the Huns," painted by Kaul-bach, in the Gallery at Berlin, which, when dark descended on the combat, continued it in the air under the stars, they are not satisfied with pecking and clawing on the ground, but must needs fly upward simultaneously, in order, I suppose, to get, one on the top of the other, and use beak more successfully. How masculine! But where is the lady? See! there she is. She was under the rhododendron bush, waiting to extend her favour to the successful athlete. But I am no wiser than ever, and I fear I must rest satisfied with maiden meditations."

'You are so discursive, Lamia, this morning," I said, ' I am quite unable to follow your reasoning."

Reasoning!" she exclaimed. As though I was ever so foolish as to reason. Of all the passions, reason is the most misleading. Do you want an authority for that statement? Then, here it is:

Reason, by reason proved unreasonable, Continues reasoning still.

See, another fight, but this time the combatants are blackbirds. Fighting is only the most conclusive form of reasoning. And now I want some violets."

Need I say that off I went, at once, to bring her some. We have them in myriads just now, but for the most part in frames, though, after a couple of sunny days, there are always some long-stalked, single Princess of Wales' in the open. By the time I had accomplished my errand, and returned with a posy of Parma ones for Lamia, the Poet was with her. She held them towards him to smell, and then fastened them just where they ought to have been, on her breast.

' How much sweeter," said the Poet, ' English violets always seem than Roman ones; as though they were lineally descended from, and had inherited the qualities of such as have been gathered for hundreds of years by English children in peaceful English lanes, or by English lads and lasses in English gardens, with exchanged blushings, and stammerings, and secluded embraces; innocent darlings of the Spring in innocent hands from innocent, but somewhat inarticulate hearts. One has gathered many a handful in the Campagna hard by the tomb of Cecilia Metella. But somehow they always seemed to smell of blood and fever; the successors of those rank with the life-stream of assassinated Emperors and lustful Empresses, or trodden under the hoofs of Goth, Gaul, and Hun."

Let no one suppose that because, in the precincts of the garden that we love, cultivated violets abound, we have frames, ' houses," conservatories, and what not, without number. On the contrary, I have never found any, save ourselves, to understand how so relatively lavish a result is produced out-of-doors by such meagre resources in ' glass." You know the old saying, ' His head will never save his legs'; but our head I am too modest to say whose head mostly saves us from much expenditure that is profitless and useless, save to enable self-indulgent gardeners to potter under cover when the weather without is not to their taste. Two diminutive houses, one of them rarely warmed artificially above a temperature needed for keeping out the frost, a few frames and pits, and an absolutely unheated peach-house useful for ' hardening off' things in the Spring, and giving us an ample supply of peaches and nectarines in

August, are our only expedients for such success as we have in the garden, and for cultivating the more delicate chrysanthemums, Arum lilies," Bride ' gladioli, and such like, to be brought indoors for decoration in December and the two following months. Between two of the peach trees, there is quite a small cluster of Iris stylosa, which is the most floriferous plant I have ever seen, and provides us with an uninterrupted succession of blooms when frosty nights keep the long out-of-door border of them in subjection. Nor must I forget, for it would be ungrateful to do so, to include in this enumeration a mode of growing violets everybody that sees them admires, but somehow never imitates. If you happen to grow violets in frames, as you probably do, you know that, all the Summer through till late September or early October when you lift them to place them in the frames, the runners must be carefully and continuously plucked off. But by leaving these on the ' Tsar' or ' Princess of Wales," and planting single roots in large pots early in November, and keeping them on a staging in the cool peach-house, we contrive to have in March a perfect forest of violet flowers, not only crowning and covering the top of the pot, but hanging down all round it in cascades a couple of feet long. I see four of them on the window-sill as I write these lines, and they are a joy to behold. I should be sorry to have to count the flowers on any one of them; and some incredulous persons, when I tell them each pot contains only one plant, go closer and, while politely pretending to be wholly lost in admiration, are scrutinising to discover whether it is so, or I am the dupe of my gardeners and my self-complacent optimism. However, seeing is believing, and they turn away from the window, employing eulogistic adjectives somewhat in excess of any even I should use. The vituperators of English Springs either live in London and have for their experience in March only hat-assailing winds and dust-storms worthy of the Sahara, and have no garden of their own; or, if they have, they do not come near it till the end of July, or they have such extensive ones that the delight of close and loving observation is unknown to them. Spring is out-and-away the most interesting time of the gardening year. Just as some of the shyer birds will sing lustily till you come near them, but suspend their carolling till you have passed, and then resume their warbling more liberally than ever, so I declare there are Spring flowers that pause in their progress if you stand and look at them, but begin growing again when you have turned your back. Daffodils behave themselves in this manner, and, late as they are this year, I will be bound to say that, in ten days' time, they will be abreast of the season. Yesterday I counted some eighty big groups of them under the oak and in the adjoining orchard, independently, of course, of those in the beds and borders. Everything is worth looking at or watching when one is approaching the vernal equinox. The first celandine, the first daisy, the earliest Siberian Scylla, the most precocious white violets, give a charm to outdoor garden life that tempts to wise idleness, as the Poet pathetically calls it when he is accused of doing nothing, and Lamia is helping him to do it.

' We leave Veronica and you alone," says Lamia, ' when she is ordering luncheon and you are balancing your accounts. So, as one good turn deserves another, leave us alone in our loitering raptures."

As a fact, Veronica I will say nothing about myself has her own closely observant rounds, generally followed by an exhortation to ' wake up ' that affords conclusive evidence of her penetrating peregrinations. I am well aware it is the modest dimension of the garden we love that encourages and renders more easy daily and almost hourly observation. It is the very vastness of the gardens of the opulent that hinders individual interest. It is the modern way, in all things, to descant about bigness, in which all the interesting little details of life and things are submerged and lost. One is expected to fall down and worship a number of ciphers, and to be overawed by the mere mention of the word million. To all such divinities we refuse our homage; and Veronica has the courage to say that adoration of magnitude is one of the marks of semi-educated persons.

c Quite true," says the Poet, borrowing something of her daring. Half-educated persons shall I say on both sides of the Atlantic? imagine the old to be novel, the commonplace to be original, and something as ancient as the hills a modern discovery. Such persons and such nations have no Past, though I suppose they are making one. But what a Past! A Past of gramaphones, multi-millionaires, and the largest circulation in the world! I wonder what the Future of such a Past will be

Another of the delights of an English Spring is that one ever and anon, though not always I allow, can let the logs burn low on the hearth, open all the windows, and admit the notes of the exhilarating music outside. ' Exhilaration no doubt," says Lamia, resuming her observation of bird-life and conduct. The song-thrushes, storm-cocks, and blackbirds, sing loudest and longest in the early morning and late evening, and most appropriately. They chant battle-songs, trumpet-calls, sound fighting fifes and flutes, stimulating courage, and defying the foe. When these cease of a morning, the battle begins, and is carried on all through the day. When twilight arrives, the combatants draw off to their tents in the trees, and shout insolent paeans of victory. You like to persuade yourself they are love-songs sung expressly by masculine devotion to soothe and amuse the poor dear things otherwise engaged, sitting patiently on their nests. Don't you believe it. It is not the habit of males anywhere to behave in any such way."

' But surely I have heard you say the contrary; and I should be astonished if your pattern poet has not pledged himself to that opinion, in verse."

' Verse pledges a man to nothing," she replied. And, as for me, have I not told you more than once, that I believe a great many things I know to be not true?"

With this closing remark, Lamia left me to my meditations, and found the Poet among the crocuses and now rapidly unsheathing daffodils under the oak; and, with him she will indulge, I have little doubt, in the sentiment she refuses to share with me. In justice to them, however, I must allow that, whenever some interesting rural sound or sight arrests their attention, they pause in their sympathetic dialogues, and devote to it minute attention. I can see from here what has attracted it at this moment. A couple of sparrow-hawks have settled on a Douglas pine near the oak. There! Away they go; far too wary to trust to the society of murderous man, though it is murder they themselves are bent on, the intended victims being the wood-pigeons that have during the last year or two ventured much nearer to the house and garden than usual, I cannot say why, unless it be that they are increasing in number, and are being crowded out in their accustomed resort in the neighbouring but a little farther off elms. They will assuredly find little enough provender in the kitchen-garden, for everything they could attack is protected by pea-guards. As I have said, many austerely devout lovers object to being married in Lent, but the partridges entertain no such scruple, pairing between them being one of the most interesting incidents of the austere season, and one is continually interrupting their honeymoon. As for the rooks at the back of the house, they are lapsing into comparative quiet, for they have finished their furnishing arrangements, during the making whereof they kept up continuous consultations, which Lamia declares remind her of certain chatterings, as she calls them, when Veronica has summoned the maids to pull the furniture about, and give the rooms, as she thinks, a wholly new appearance. On these occasions, the Poet and I get into sad trouble, for we always fail to observe the important transformation that has taken place, and get soundly rated for our lack of observation. Yet, out-of-doors, I think we are both observant enough. The other day, when it was suggested that those same sparrow-hawks were probably seeing where they would set up house the suggestion proceeded from one of that half of the population who are always anxious to bring on other folks' nuptials as quickly as possible the Poet observed that sparrow-hawks do not nest before June, probably from the evolved instinct that they need, for safe domestic arrangements, as dense a leaf covering and protection as possible in the woods hard-by that we continually wander in.

For let no one suppose that we ourselves are garden gaol-birds, and never get beyond self-complacent strolls round and round our narrow precincts. During the last month, the woods have been a daily haunt with us; for the woodlanders have been hard at work, and I know no more picturesque rural industry than theirs. It is so clean-looking, so wholesome, so illustrative of the many-sided craft of rustic industry. And every dozen years or so it opens out the lie of the ground where it takes place, and lets one see the ups-and-downs of tracts at other times concealed under a certain look of uniformity. The timber, of course, is left alone till May, but everything else is cleared, and material is obtained for a dozen different useful purposes. There are the tall straight hop-poles to begin with. Then there are the ' use-poles," cut into all sorts and sizes for stakes and ' binders." The material for the making of hurdles is set apart, and everything, till carted away, is stacked on the ground in the most orderly fashion. If you are a townsman and, if you are, I have little doubt you think you know everything do you know what a spile-fence' is?

' I know no such word in the English language," said a highly educated, townsman to me the other day, when I named it. ' I suppose it is a local word," he added, a touch contemptuously.

' Let us look in the dictionary," I said, with the becoming humility of the rustic.

We looked, and there the word was, as large as life, and its rootship with ' pile," with which my urban companion was acquainted, was duly set down. Spile-fences have come much into fashion about us of late. They are made of narrow but substantial stakes of split wood, pointed and driven firmly into the ground at about a couple of inches apart, and linked together near the top by strong wire. They look very neat, and are perfectly effectual for a good many years. Then we must not forget the pea-sticks, for peas both edible and sweet, or those important things in the season of the Winter months, faggots for lighting fires and heating ovens. This is a fairly long catalogue of usefulness in the work of woodlanders, which likewise ministers to beauty as well as to utility. Wherever a wood is now being cleared in the manner I have described, next

Spring the ground will be a forest of primroses, wind-flowers, and bluebells. Then then every recurring year, surely it is true as ever of the primroses:

First you came by ones and ones, Lastly in battalions. Skirmish along hedge and bank, Turn old Winter's wavering flank, Round his flying footsteps hover, Seize on hollow, ridge, and cover, Leave nor slope nor hill unharried, Till, his snowy trenches carried, O'er his sepulchre you laugh, Winter's joyous epitaph.

EVEN if, as I say, you are a townsman, and possess the superior intelligence that one well knows is an urban monopoly, you will surely not deny that the labourers who do the woodland work I have just described cannot be wholly unintelligent. They have no machinery to help them in it, to save them trouble and the effort of thinking. Every stroke of it has to be thought over. Completely to train a man how to do it is impossible, though much can be learnt in that way. For woods vary; trees vary; undergrowth varies. Part of it has to be treated in one way, part in another. It cannot be performed by the hard-and-fast rule of any science, unless scientific ' be taken in its simpler meaning of knowing and understanding. It allows a certain latitude of judgment, and will, and choice to the worker; and that is why it is so welcome to, and so efficiently performed by,

English folk versed in this branch of woodcraft. For an Englishman is never so thoroughly an Englishman as when he is in a fresh position, particularly if it be a difficult one. ' Leave me alone, and let me do it my own way." That is our native way of facing difficulties, more especially if there be something new and unforeseen in it; and so we ' muddle through," in peace no less than in war. But we do muddle through, and come out on the far side, neither beaten nor baffled, as we have seen happen to some scientific nations, in presence of the unexpected. So Woodlanders, and indeed rustics generally, are not so wanting in intelligence, after all.

I submitted the foregoing remarks to the Poet, and asked him if he thought them true or the reverse.

' Absolutely true," he replied; ' and since you ask for my opinion, I will give it frankly. Rustic labourers are not only fully as intelligent as town artisans, but more so. They say less, but they reflect more. In their long silences, they are pondering, in a slow, draught-horse sort of way; but they are getting over the road carefully and continuously, and on to the end of it. The rural mind thinks for itself, and by itself; the workers in towns think collectively, if such can properly be called thinking. They move each other, not by reflection, but by emotion and impulse. Their judgment often gets intoxicated by some effervescing and frothy orator; reminding one of what was said of a well-known political leader now no more, by a friendly commentator of his own party, that he resembled second-rate champagne in a first-rate state of effervescence. They are influenced by invectives and gibes in the newspapers they read. They attend closely to their work; but much of it is, so to speak, wound up for them beforehand, and they and it go like a watch or a pianola. That deadens rather than sharpens observation, and cannot possibly minister to the active employment of the faculties of the thinking kind. The hedger, ditcher, thatcher, catcher, is continually asking himself, for he is forced to do so, "How is this to be done? " Ditches differ; straw for thatching is not always of the same length or the same substance. Some hedges are young, some middle-aged, some old, some well-furnished, others in places very bare. Cart-horses are not without a mind of their own, and are not to be trusted. It is easy enough to get the town workman to talk, but he will pay you with words, as the French say, and repeat newspaper to you by the furlong. He is a machine driven by other machines. The rustic, even when he knows you well, and feels kindly and trustfully towards you, is slow of speech, for there is no sudden electric communication between his brain and his tongue. The two communicate with each other slowly and at a foot's pace. But he says nothing, when he has nothing to say; and, when he has something to say, says it without exaggeration or excessive emphasis, and he listens to what you urge or object with attentive but critical ears. Disraeli observed, in his Life of Lord George Eentinck that Sir Robert Peel could play on the House of Commons as on an old fiddle, and make it dance and jig to his bowing. A sonorous rhetorician can do pretty much the same with average town audiences, unless his observations run absolutely counter to their prejudices. The same speaker is listened to by an assembly of rustics without interruption, without cheers, and without any audible enthusiasm; and he returns to his club in Pall Mall and vows he never addressed such stupid people in his life before. In reality, it is he, not they, that are stupid. They both listened and understood, and went home, in ones, twos, or threes; and, after having thought it all over, probably without a word to their wives about it, discussed it quietly, and with but a small vocabulary, on the morrow, with each other. They vote when election time comes in just the same way, each man according as he himself thinks. They do not walk to the poll imposingly, in newspaper parlance, five hundred strong, all of one mind, but independently and alone. If that does not show superior intelligence, my idea of intelligence must be sadly astray."

Do you think," I asked, ' there is any connection between this contrast of the rural and the urban mind, and the contrast which is to be observed between Parliamentary representatives drawn from a class more closely connected with the country and the soil, and those whose lives have been spent more exclusively in towns, in trade and manufactures?"

' Unquestionably," he replied, ' I should say; and, as I have no intention of standing for an electoral constituency, I can afford to be frank and say exactly what I think. The contrast is marked, and the advantage for practical purposes and the welfare of the State is on the side of the rural class. They seem to me to look at legislation with the eyes and judgment of statesmanship.

Town-bred representatives, as a rule, are political rather than statesmanlike. Our wisest public men have belonged to the former, by origin, training, and taste. We have had prominent public men belonging to the other class, very clever, very brilliant, very energetic, very commanding, if you like, but scarcely wise. If you think Lord Beaconsfield was an exception, and contradicts what I am saying, is it not accurate to reply that, while in origin he belonged to neither, his temperament, his affections, his habits, were from the very first of the country sort? Gifted with an active imagination, he employed it practically to what are called practical affairs; in other words, to politics, his conduct in which was dictated by a knowledge of human nature and history. Unimaginative men failed for a long time to understand him, but ended by seeing that he towered above them all in statesmanship by virtue of this union of the imaginative and the practical. I fear that the men who are neither imaginative nor practical, but theorisers and sciolists, are at present in the ascendant. If they have their own way, unchecked, they will ruin an ancient Realm and destroy a great Empire. I will go yet farther, and avow the opinion that the House of Lords, as a body, are wiser and more statesmanlike than the House of Commons, taken as a body. The former debate, the latter harangue. Whenever I have attended a discussion in the Lords, I felt that, though it was conducted with an almost total absence of eloquence, nearly every one that spoke spoke to the point, and whether I happened to agree or not, was addressing me and persons like me, with reasons I could at least understand. From a debate in the House of Commons I have generally come away with the impression that most of the speakers were talking over my head to the " man-in-the-street," and by no means the sanest and soundest minded in it."

Lamia had joined us during the latter part of the foregoing; and when there came a pause, she took the opportunity of saying: ' I am glad such are your sentiments, for they would leave you at the bottom of the poll in any urban constituency in the kingdom; so one need not be afraid lest we should all be condemned to live in town during the loveliest and most interesting of the seasons, while you had a latch-key with which to let yourself in when there had been an all-night series of divisions among the sons of the Mother of Parliaments."

' Small fear of that," said Veronica, who was now of the company. I can scarcely imagine the author of an unpublished invective in verse I read the other day against the Time, for those special evils and omens that are fostered and flourish by it, thanks to the particular form of civilisation that is daily hailed with a paean in newspapers and nightly on popular platforms in the House of-Commons, doing anything of the kind."

When," asked Lamia, ' are you going to publish it for the benefit of those concerned?"

Are you referring to Cassandra Speaks?" he asked. ' If so, never! Just as one may justifiably think a thing without saying it, so one may excusably write what one would justly be reproached for publishing. A philippic, whether in verse or prose, against an Age is pretty much in the same category as an indictment against an entire nation; and you know what Burke said of that. A shrewd man of the world once observed, when some one showed him a letter intended for the post, and asked him his opinion of it. " It is the best letter," he replied, "I ever read. And now throw it into the fire." The evils of society are not to be remedied, or the mania of an age arrested, by denunciations either in verse or prose. Where the break is to come from to check the accelerating movement of material civilisation, I own I do not see; but it is no use crying out " Stop, stop!" to persons who are going too fast, but are so delighted and self-satisfied in making such a clatter by their progress that they do not even hear you. Moreover, along with the mischief and dangers, or what one believes to be such, you are referring to, efforts of the noblest, most touching, and most disinterested kind are being made to meet and mitigate their baneful effect; and, unless accompanied by recognition of these, wholesale denunciation necessarily seems one-sided and partial. I know there are persons who read a slashing satire or a sonorous philippic solely as a work of Art, and enjoy it simply as such. But years bring a semi-indulgent attitude towards people and things one cannot admire, though perhaps such an attitude is merely a sign of the indecision, moral no less than mental, of age."

' I suppose so," said Veronica. But I read two sonnets the other day which, it seemed to me, represent that conflict in the mind that may sometimes arise without its incurring the reproach of indecision. I allude to " Monastery Bells." ' ' I was thinking of them," said Lamia, ' all the time we were talking."

' You may repeat them," said Veronica, ' if you happen to remember them."

' Since you bid me," said Lamia, ' I will do so.

MONASTERY BELLS

Sometimes when, weary, the sad soul rebels Against the strife and discord all around, One seems to catch the faint and far-off sound Of melody that softly sinks and swells. It is the sound of Monastery Bells, In solitudes by Sanctuary crowned, From meditation peaceful and profound Calling grave Friars to prayer from silent cells. Then yearningly one craves to have release From the crowd's rivalries and worthless prize, To find some spot where Glory's selfish sighs And struggle's endless tribulations cease, To join in Vespers' chant as sunset dies, And pass life's evening in monastic peace.

But when resound, as day dawns dim and drear, Meanings of anguish, sobbings of distress, From heartless homes of famished loneliness, With none to rescue, nothing to revere, Again one feels one still is wanted here, To aid, admonish, comfort, and caress, Smooth the rough pillow pallid sufferers press, Stanch the fresh wound, and wipe away the tear.

So, though one longs as ever to depart,
And to gross sounds and sighs live deaf and blind,
Sorrowing one stays with sorrow, still resigned
To work, unhired, amid life's hireling mart,
To cherish in the crowd monastic mind,
And in a world profane a cloistered heart."

Lady Day. When things have been kept back, as we say in gardening language, by a lagging Spring, cold if not cruel nights, and absence of encouraging showers, what a rapid start forward they make and how they hurry along when they have once begun to wake up and open their eyes on an expectant and well-prepared world. That is what has happened this year. We have felt nothing of

Amazonian March with breast half bare, And sleety arrows whistling through the air, but a March more like a mild February, crying a halt rather than repeating its own name to mustering volunteers of the borders and shrubberies. There is something at once characteristic and delightful in the unpunctuality of the earlier period of the twelvemonth. Is it calculated capriciousness, or only easy-going indifference? Who shall say? Spring is an incorrigible coquette, and I suppose that is why she enchants us so. That on Lady Day the crocuses under the oak, yellow, white, purple, lilac, in most admired disorder, should only now be beginning to wane, is unprecedented in one's now pretty long experience of times and seasons; and it is equally beyond my remembrance that, shortly before such a date, one should have been looking for daffodils that had not yet opened. But they are here now, though not in abundance. In a few days more, however, they will be; and the association of crocuses and daffodils, side by side in one plot of turf a hundred feet by seventy, under the overbranching oak, is a sight quite new to me. To-day is so warm that ever and anon one has not been able to resist the temptation to sit on the freshly-put-out garden-seats which, by the bye, Veronica says want varnishing very badly and listen to the perpetual cawing of the rooks, on household cares intent, to use the Mil tonic language which Taine says the author of Paradise Lost on such occasions employs, as though Eden had been an English middle-class home where of a Sunday respectable people dine at one o'clock. What they are saying, one no more really knows than one can decipher the Etruscan tongue; though probably, as Lamia suggests, they are ' talking shop," like the rest of the world, and making such a fuss over the building of a few nests. Then one starts up again, curious to see if merle and mavis, that are singing so jubilantly, have likewise been furnishing, and on the way comes across a blue egg with brownish spots lying on the ground, and draws one's own conclusions. It is the season of seasons for the nuptials of partridges, blackbirds, missel- thrushes, finches, hedge-sparrows, and the rest of the tribe now revelling in their honeymoon, passing their lune de miel at home, while in like circumstances we go off on our travels, some of us for the first time abroad.

April i. Far from exaggerating, I have underrated the agreeable results of such hitherto unknown tardiness in the first intimations of Spring. The most delightful of them is the introduction to each other of flowers that, as far as my observation goes, have hitherto been strangers, not even ' on nodding terms. I verily believe the crocuses under the oak intended all the time to remain in beauty, if waningly, till All Fools' day, if only for once to see the daffodils, single, double, deep yellow, pale coloured, as well as the little dwarf ones, the tags (for I know no other name for them); and even a tulip or two, and a lovely clump of dwarf iris, whose name I believe to be Iris histrio) though I am not quite sure, deep blue, freckled with brilliant gold spots, are sunning themselves with the utmost self-complacency. The pale blue Anemone Apennina, which they sell in basketfuls in Rome about this season, are showing flower under the wall of the Poet's Corner; and in a day or two the Crown Imperials will make a gallant show of royal precocity. Lest, however, you should be led to imagine that no misfortunes ever happen in the garden that I love, let me make a distressing confession. In two long beds the yellow Pottebakker tulips have come to utter grief; and I am driven to conclude that either they are too delicate to stand such frosts as we had a little while back, or some subterranean enemy hath done this, when I examine the still perfectly solid bulbs but imperfect flower-sheaths. As they were to flower along with the blue forget-me-not, the gap will be a standing sorrow from the middle of the month till the end of May. Trying to make the best of a bad business, I have sent the gardeners to a neighbouring wood to dig up primrose roots, whose lateness in flowering this year I have recorded, and they must replace the tulips that have ' gone home." But I know Veronica will lead me a life about them, attributing their failure to some malefic influence of my own, greatly to the satisfaction of Lamia, who loves to see me in trouble, and somewhat to the amusement of the philosophic Poet.

May Day. May Day this year ought to be ashamed of itself. A procession, field festival, and prize-giving, all in the open air, had been arranged in our nearest and avowedly picturesque village for to-day, and it has rained without intermission from dawn to dusk. The lap of May has indeed been chilled by a lingering imitation of winter, and white frocks, neat stockings, and smart little hats have been bedraggled by wind and wet. A learned Pope apparently all Popes do not conform to the general English opinion that they are ignorant and superstitious fanatics, even when not something worse set the world right in the sixteenth century in regard to the heavenly calendar; and though, since the information proceeded from so tainted a source, our own enlightened country was slow to accept it, and did not do so till 1752, we found ourselves at last forced by a world actually as civilised and progressive as ourselves to do so. The supposed most brilliant monarch of to-day, a certain well-known Continental Emperor, has sought to rival, if not to outshine, poor benighted Pope Gregory by proclaiming 1900 to be the first year of the twentieth century in the most approved modern American language, the ' Twent-Cent." But the Edict has not been deferred to; though, save in Russia, the Gregorian Calendar now rules throughout Christendom. Yet the twelve days' anticipation of former dates it necessitated has been attended by some non-astronomical drawbacks. Even grave historians and essayists have been betrayed into curious blunders in some of their dates and footnotes, with the result that the alert critic, eager to air that superior knowledge indispensable to the pursuit of his calling, has pounced down on them with traditional scorpions, and flogged away to his heart's content. What is somewhat more important, at least in the eyes of the occupants of the Garden that we love, is the topsy-turvydom the altered calendar often causes in the rustic mind. It will probably be news to those of our omniscient urban parliamentary representatives who have all sorts of remedial proposals for land tenure, while knowing as much about it as they do of the satellites of Mars, that rural Quarter-days on which rents are paid are not those to be found in fpMtaker's Almanac or Acts of Parliament, but fall twelve days later; the rustic mind, which of course is always behindhand, a wiser and less dangerous thing than being a little previous," still going with his rent in his hand not on March 25, but on April 6, and not on September 29, but on October n, often receiving a reduction in its amount from a sympathetic landlord, which is more than I ever heard of being given, save of other people's money, by the most benevolent ' advanced' owner of house property in cities.

' What very irrelevant observations!" the latter will doubtless say, should he condescend to read these pages, with a fine House-of-Commons wave of the hand. But to the more open minds of the country-side the observation will seem pertinent enough, though not in a cut-and-dried fashion. Had the ruling spirit of the May procession and the rest waited till May 13 for the holding of the Children's Festival, he would probably have fared better. But, though a really worthy person, I fear he has got most of his ideas from books, not from personal experience of the seasons; in this respect somewhat resembling other watchful critics, who go on taxing English poets that extol the vernal season with having got their notions concerning it from Theocritus and other literary southern sources, and not from real and actual experience, notwithstanding the amiable retort of a poet in his ' A Defence of English Spring," when the specious reproof was first addressed to Spring-loving versifiers.

May 11. Never was the transforming power of the sun shown more surprisingly than during the last three days. The under-average temperature that had so long prevailed and retarded vegetation has suddenly been altered to above-average temperature still more remarkable; and the Garden that I love, and the parks, commons, and woodlands round it, have all expanded into a scene of intoxicating loveliness. How is it possible to repress the observation, born not of complacency, but of love and the desire to share all good things with others, ' I wish all the world were here to see it!" An Italian, gazing on it, would exclaim, ' Oh! che belluria!" which is not adequately rendered into English by ' O what beauty!" or by ' How beautiful!" but rather by What beautifulness! ' For it is the fulness, the reckless bounty and lavishness, that makes it all so wonderful. Two of the Pyrus Malus, as big and bushy as large hawthorn trees, are smothered in blossom; and others, less large, but some of still deeper colour, bear them in company. Do these, or the double Japanese cherry trees, both white and rose-colour, deserve the prize for efflorescent splendour? Nor is the gold-flowering berberis to be outdone by them, and adds to its unequalled sheen the attraction of penetrating perfume. Towering above them is a tree it is more like a white fountain than a tree called a Bird Cherry. The but enough, perhaps already overmuch, of panegyric, and I will try to introduce a note of depreciation, though it is difficult where everything in general looks so beautiful. Though the birds keep singing incessantly, I have noticed that the lambs have bleated this year much less than usual. I suspect it is that they bleat when they are uncomfortable and cold, or want something or other they have not got. Lamia suggests that no one makes a noise who is perfectly contented, and that even poets, on the authority of one of them, learn in suffering what they teach in song.

' As witness ours!" I said somewhat sardonically.

I quite understand your insinuation," Lamia replied. 'But how can you, or I, or any one tell? Poor fellow, he too may have been cradled into poetry by wrong, though how, when, or where, I allow, does not appear. And perhaps it never happened at all."

' Likely enough," I said, or to any of the musically miserable race. Probably the tradition is only a poetic fiction."

' Possibly," added Lamia, with unusual assent to a suggestion of mine. ' There is nothing more utterly misleading than translating poetic fictions into realistic prose. Yet let us not forget we have been told that, as the sun draws up the mists of the valley to the mountain tops, to melt them to ether,

So the effulgent mind

Can call up sorrow to its own great height, To dissipate it there.

' And what says the wisest, as the greatest of all poets?

Shall we rest us here, And, by narrating tales of others' griefs, See if 'twill teach us to forget our own.

Does not that explain a good many things in this world that might otherwise be unintelligible?"

May 30. Lest it should be thought that we are so wedded to our Garden that we never leave it, I may recall that we have recently paid a visit to the northern coast of Somerset and Devon, to spots familiar of old to the Poet, in days concerning which we ask only discreet questions, but not before visited by the other denizens of the Garden that we love. With a rare freedom from local prejudice, he has often said that the West of England is much superior to the East, more picturesque, more various, more musical, for it abounds in streams, bounding torrents, and winding rivers, in which the Home Counties are sadly wanting.

'Nor are these its only advantages," he goes on to say; 'it is more primitive, more simple in its ways, still uninfluenced, save in one or two much-frequented watering-places, by the malefic example of London, its monotonous luxury, extravagance, and feverish yearning for artificial pleasure. And then, Veronica," he crowns all by saying, ' it is much cheaper ' Let us put all this to the test," was the triple reply; and so westward we went.

There was a consensus of opinion as we began to get deeper into western scenery. What an undulating world! What greenery! What lush-ness! What twisting, rippling, happy, dimpling streams! See, see! there are the otter hounds at work, and country folk of all sorts afoot after them! How we should have liked to pull the check-string of the railway carriage and get down and run across the intervening mead and join the amphibious chase! And the hills, the dense sloping woodlands, the richness of vegetation and prospect everywhere! Lamia produced one of the Poet's fishing-fly books, and held it up to him with a significant gesture. But he checked her enthusiasm.

Yes, Lamia, there are trout in all these streams, far more than in our sluggish water at home, but they are much smaller, and afford much poorer sport than our one, two, three-pounders. But everything else is better here l Except the Garden," I pleaded humbly.

Don't be too sure of that," said Veronica. I should think that, for gardening, this is an even better sort of Ireland in many ways, and we know what that is."

' Perhaps including its untidiness," I rejoined, not to be outdone.

A plague on gardens," exclaimed Lamia. ' Are we never to get away from them? These woods and meadows and rambling, laughing, irresponsible waters are worth all the gardens in the world, even when written about and illustrated."

We were making for as primitive a place as there is in the Island, probably the most primitive of all the places answering to the wants of a simple but reasonably refined life, and reached it early in the evening, after a nine miles' drive from the nearest station.

' This is as far as I can go," said our driver; 'you must please to walk down to the village."

Very cautiously on the part of Veronica, very recklessly on that of Lamia, the slippery stones of the broad stair-steps down to the village were descended, till we reached the top of a narrow village street of picturesque old-world cottages, that still kept dipping down in the same fashion, to a diminutive port at the bottom. All the little houses had small, but well-stocked, gardens in front of them, and half-way along them there was an inn, whose sign-board swayed in the breeze on the upper balcony. Our ' things' were brought down in well-balanced panniers on donkeys, whose iron-shod feet sounded pleasantly on the round, slippery stones, and the Poet said it reminded him of his boyhood, not in the West, but in the North, of England, where there were thatched cottages and oatcake, and a silvery snow-cold torrent sang adown what was called the village street, and declared the world was a better world then than in days of motor-cars, grand cosmopolitan hotels, and foreign waiters. Our reception was by a deaf old lady, who dropped us a curtsey as in the days of the Armada, duly recognised by Veronica and Lamia with a friendly handshake, and by the Poet with one of his finest salutations, the old lady's married daughter, and their smiling handmaidens. Having been shown our white-curtained rooms, the various approaches to which were by up-and-down steps perilous to incautious movements, we were told dinner would be ready for us as soon as ever we wished, but over the way, down the inn steps across the narrow street, and up some fresh ones. Lamia declared she was as hungry as a whole hunting-field, in a voice that would have created an appetite in the most dyspeptic, and we are none of us that. We fell to with a will to a meal welcome in its perfect simplicity, everything being piping hot though fetched from across the street, except the cold stewed gooseberries and Devonshire cream at the end of our repast.

'What could the unvitiated palate or unde-moralised man wish for more?" asked the Poet. ' But the line must always be drawn somewhere; and I advise you, Veronica, not to ask for coffee."

When we woke the following morning, we found the narrow, long street festooned with flags, and inquired what was going to happen. We were told that a county celebrity who had never been there was staying at the Court with the owner of the village and all the country round, and that, as everybody wished to see him, he would probably walk up or down its boulder-paved way. In the course of the morning he did so; and, as we happened to have some acquaintance with him, and were sitting in the inn balcony as he passed, he stopped to have a little talk with us, and made the owner just referred to and us acquainted; and the result was we were hospitably loz THE GARDEN THAT I LOVE made free of all the more private drives and walks in the neighbourhood.

See!" said the Poet, ' what comes of patriarchal government, so much abused in these enlightened days. There is no colossal hotel, for such would not be tolerated by the benighted and unbeknighted owner of the place, no rush of curious, indifferent tourists, flourishing their finery or blowing their horns for six hours at the seaside, but only water-colour painters with their unpretentious easels placed wherever it suits the artist to place them, poets humming to themselves, and quiet, deliberate thinkers. Thank Heaven! there are still a few such places left."

We quitted the sheltered backwater with silent regret, Veronica reminding us that we had engaged rooms in the same county at a spot which the Poet had declared, before he left home, combined the most varied scenery with the fullest union of beauty and majesty of any in the United Kingdom, if exception were made of Killarney and Glengariff. As we approached it, I could see he manifested a certain anxiety as to whether it would be thought he had drawn a somewhat long draft on the deposit book of imaginative memory. But it turned out quite otherwise. Lamia was glowingly silent, and

Veronica rapturously admiring, as we passed into the garden of a comparatively small hotel with a lowly roof and name, and, over flowering trees and shrubs which, were I honest, which I cannot possibly be on such a subject, I should perhaps allow outdid those of a certain other garden, gazed down on to the open sea, along a magnificent coast line, and then up to wooded hills and wild moorland, while rippling music reached us from an unseen torrent somewhere not far away. There were many signs of advanced civilisation, as compared with the rickety old place of the age of the Armada, evidently not wholly unwelcome to Veronica.

So far so good. But after an exploration of a most enchanting kind, a bell rang, and it was dinner time. A Continental male waiter of spotless garments, faultless manners, and evidently much capacity, showed us to our table, rather as though it were a pew; and then there slowly streamed in to the other tables a number of as respectable-looking persons, mostly of the more impeccable sex, as I ever saw.

Oh! ' gasped Lamia, which elicited a rebuking shake of the head from Veronica, and a smile behind his unfolded napkin from the Poet.

Do you think they have all been to church?"

asked Lamia, unobservant of Veronica's admonition.

You forget it is not Sunday," I said.

' Not at all," she replied. Respectable people do not confine their devotions to one day in the week. Is it Lent?"

' On the contrary," said the Poet, catching from her the spirit of revolt," it is Whitsun week, a week of rejoicing."

' Then let us rejoice," cried Lamia, though I fear that will make us rather exclusive."

' I wonder what they are like when they are at home," said the Poet.

' I know," said Lamia, ' for I once saw them, and to the best advantage, for it was Sunday afternoon, which, as I have said, I know this is not. I have heard it stated that good Americans, when they die, go to Paris, though I believe they now come to London. Wicked English people, while still alive, are sent from Saturday to Monday to Tonbridge Wells. That is how I came to be there."

The Poet, growing worse and worse, indeed absolutely fearless, told her that if she did not behave better, he felt sure she would be sent upstairs to dine by herself. The following day she did not appear at luncheon till it was quite over, and then declared she had been unable to meet so many well-behaved people three times a day, and had enjoyed some stewed gooseberries and Devonshire junket in her own room. But when the day arrived for our departure, we all felt a pang at leaving such a magnificent medley of Nature's stern, sweet, lofty, and lordly aspects, resounding streams and silent mountains, indented coast and crags fronting a channel broad enough to be mistaken for the open sea. And now that we are at home again, we recall only our enjoyment, and, according to the kindly dispensation under which we live, even Lamia quite forgot the irreproachable deportment of uncongenial British respectability.

Midsummer Day. While not allowing that either we or our neighbours have done anything to be entitled to fine weather, I must say that I never before saw so ill-conducted a May and June. Days of sunlessness and showers have been followed by gloomy twilights and cold nights. Yet neither bird nor bloom has taken notice of the cheerlessness of the season. Song-thrush and blackbird, blackcap and garden warbler, have lived, loved, and chanted as jubilantly as ever; and I must be forgiven for saying, since it is the bare truth, that this, I daresay, over-belauded Garden has never before been more agreeable to the eye. At this moment it is a forest of flowers, crowning lavish leafage, of faultless form, uninjured colour, and growth of unprecedented lushness. Do not expect from me the enumeration of rare plants and recondite flowers. Did I not once say that I see no reason why a garden should be either a museum or a hospital, though, rightly enough, places are kept apart for these by the botanically inclined. Ours is still, and is likely to remain, what a now penitent lady called an ignorant garden; full of common things for the common eye and heart, but, as far as I have observed, as good and thriving of their kind as are to be found anywhere. There are irises, from four inches to four feet high. Many are between those extreme measurements; the Spanish irises blend with the two-year-old French tea-roses blessings on la belle France if only for its roses! and among the first-year-flowering China ones, Laurette Messimy for choice, with its ruby-coloured stems and buds and ineffably beautiful if fragile blooms, the annual Marguerite carnations promise to flower as profusely as ever. The Quaker-maid Violas, for the original strain of which we have to thank Mr. Speaker, who, I should think, longs to leave the Chair for his terraces in the North, not occupied by tea-tables and, one would have thought, rather unsuitable guests for a serious, if it be any longer a serious, House of Commons, but with secular yew-trees, have done splendidly as a broad edging round the rose-beds; and, by dint of constant picking off of the seeding flowers, they prolong their stay for four months. Creeper and larkspur, the latter of every imaginable shade of blue, clematis and pœony poppy clamber so as to be conspicuously seen; a Frogmore Anchusa italica, Anglice Alkanet, of the Boragewort tribe, and the smaller and finer perpetual Verbascum, lavender-coloured Erigeron or Fleabane, dwarfer but many branching annual sunflowers, and well-contented Love-in-a-Mist, would all sun themselves if they could, but contrive wonderfully well to do without the sunshine that has so long been due. Several visitors have said that our Love-in-the-Mist is of a deeper blue than theirs, and beg for seed, which of course they can have in any quantity, though we have our doubts about the greater deepness of the blue, or attribute it to wiser cultivation of some kind.

Do you cry, Enough! enough!" and shall I change the subject? I will directly, for Lamia is coming this way and doubtless will change it for me. But, before I do so, I want to pay homage to the roses from the foot to the corner of the house; much-improved, more vigorous, more clambering descendants of the dear old matronly Gloire de Dijon, the William Allen Richardson which I prefer to call the Apricot Rose, the large single white ones, the Carmine Pillar, the Maids of the Village, which, if you like the foreign lady's name, you can call Aimee Guibert, the Crimson Rambler, which, despite hasty assertions, and lugubrious prophecies, has mingled in the most friendly manner with the last, as with large white roses does the purple Clematis, and more that I have no doubt I have overlooked, or have ignored, because, however handsome they may be, they bear the name of men and women, and even princesses. No one at any rate, no man deserves to have had a rose christened by his name. Remember what Urania says in Fortunatus the Pessimist; and we all, perhaps from a little natural partiality, find her the most lovable gardener in the world.

Look on this rose

Fantastically called The Poet's Dream: Yet not without a reason, for it roams, Rambles, and climbs, no pillar, porch, nor wall Will satisfy its vagrancy; and should You try to prune its wanderings or check Its heavenward aspiration, lo! it dies. And so I let it gipsy as it will, Most careless and capricious of the roses, And therefore most desired; a rose too free To bloom in bondage.

FORTUNATUS.

O wise wilding rose! You are a fairy godmother, and well You moralise your garden.

You see I cannot stop, and, like a garrulous speaker at a public dinner, plead only one word more," which invariably turns out to be several. But tribute must be paid to the repairing power of Nature. I daresay you have forgotten, but after years of procrastination and petitioning for reprieve, the oak near the Manor Pound, that, to be truthful, never had any merit save its look of hoar antiquity, and was probably born old many generations ago, had to be condemned to be beheaded and then uprooted, lest it should commit unhappy despatch for itself, and in its suicidal no THE GARDEN THAT I LOVE compact with a fierce south wind deal destruction around as it tottered to its end. That was three years ago. We all know what is an ill wind. But three summers have come and gone; and where it stood and had a considerable space of deep shade to itself there is now one of the most sunny yet sheltered spots in the garden, where both dwarf Iris stylose and late German ones prosper amazingly, and there are yet more roses, Japanese Briars, old-world English roses, Celestial and Maiden's Blush, and, loveliest of all, after the eglantine in the hedges, a row of Penzance Briars producing wreaths, curves and festoons of colour, a perfect rainbow of scented hues.

1 1 quite agree with Veronica," says Lamia, who has now joined me with an instinctive surmise of my self-complacent raptures, 'that your' why mine? ' your Lilium auratum stalks look most unpromising. How is this?"

' You must ask the all-conquering Japanese," I replied. You cannot think worse of their appearance and prospects than I do, and I fear it comes of an excessive demand for them and the unscrupulous packing of them by those enterprising islanders, who, I am told, are rather slippery customers in commerce, before the bulbs are properly ripened off. The Poet," I went on, in order to shield myself against any further depreciation of what I am not responsible for, 4 made some suggestive observations the other day pertinent to this question ' His observations are always pertinent," she replied, and I smiled inwardly at the success of my diplomatic tact. ' I think," she went on, ' I know to what you refer. He pointed out that in all periods of transitional thought and belief the conscience suffers, since its old sanctions have been removed and none other have yet taken their place. It is undermined, without being adequately propped. Hence your measly-looking lilies from the Flowery Land. Hence, too, perhaps, my own elastic conscience, always in a state of transition. Still, I have one saving quality. I cling to my prejudices, and, by way of valuable advice, I say to you, Never give up your prejudices. They are the one last barrier between one and the utter demoralisation of one's thoughts and feelings."

I looked as grave as might be under this paradoxical peroration, and gazed into the heart of a Shirley poppy.

' Are not the poppies beautiful?" she asked: ' the fairest, the most fragile, the most fateful of all the flowers, the very type of so many women; a dainty and deadly opiate. I see the Chinese are going to shut up their opium dens. When shall we do the same with ours, and forbid the importation of the drug from No. 226 one millionth 94th Street, New Canterbury, U. S. A.? " St. Swithins Day. On this auspicious day for the conservatively reverent, or, if you like, hopefully superstitious mind, the weather has taken a turn for the better; the sun is shining with dazzling effect, and it is full summer in more than name. Flowers there were in profusion already, but the sunshine heightens their beauty, and sets off their charm as, some people would say, an ample supply of wax candles sets off other lovely creatures and their diamonds. Delighted as we are at the change, we are rather sorry for ourselves that the otherwise welcome transformation should have come when we had arranged and subscribed for three afternoon concerts in London. For, as I said just now, we are not so narrow and exclusive in our tastes as my imperfect record of our days might lead you to suppose. Lamia still enchants us from time to time with her unprofessional but native gift of song; and, in default of better, and as a musical makeshift, we have the best pianola we could find, and Veronica, with that infatuation for perfection and thoroughness with which you are acquainted, has devoted an amount of study and practice to it which enable her to extract from it all it is capable of yielding, and, of an evening, plays her favourite composer, Chopin, who is perhaps the most uniformly inspired musical man of genius since Mozart. But Music is so beloved by the Poet, and indeed by all of us, that we often go where alone, within reach, it is to be had at its very best, just for the day. He has always declared that Music is a luxurious necessity, a stimulant of the mind, and a soother of the soul, as Dante avers in the Second Canto of the Purgatorio it so often was to him also, when Casella Casellio mio, my Casella, as with grateful affection he calls him and he meet in Purgatory.

' Can you recall the lines for me, Lamia?" I asked. Thereupon, with that wonderful memory of hers, she begins:

' Ed io: Se nuova legge non ti toglie Memoria o uso all' amoroso canto Che mi solea quetar tutte mie voglie, Di ci6 ti piaccea consolare alquanto

L' anima mia, che con la sua persona Venendo qui, e affannato tanto.

Amor che nella mente mi ragiona,

Commencio egli allor si dolcemente,

Che la dolcezza ancor dentro mi suona."

' What a striking anticipation, more than six hundred years before, is that last line," I said, ' of Wordsworth's couplet:

The music in my heart I bore Long after it was heard no more."

But what, for the moment, is so illustrative of what I was urging is the yearning in the passage for the soothing power of Music, so felt by the Poet and Lamia, because, affannato tanto, so wearied by the burden of the body. Accordingly he, and therefore, of course, she, prefer Mozart to any other composer, and are always ready to do battle for his essential superiority to all other men of genius who have expressed themselves by sheer music.

' One has had to pass, in one's lifetime, through periods," he observes, ' when this estimate was regarded as a mark of one's inferiority, a reproach very easy to put up with, just as, in one's admiration of Raphael, one has gone through a similar experience. But mankind, in the long run, are sane as regards music, painting, poetry, and the other arts, just as they are, in the long run, in things political and social. There are periodical aberrations from sanity; but the high road of right reason and correct taste is by-and-by returned to."

Are we just at present," I asked, on the sane high road of judgment and feeling, or deviating from it? ' I think," he answered, one sees encouraging symptoms of a disposition to return to it, after rather long aberration. I suppose people, whose preferences repose on no thought-out principle nor conviction, but are swayed by every wind of doctrine and sentiment, get tired of just balance in the various Arts, so conspicuous in Mozart in music, notwithstanding his unfailing genius, and in Raphael in painting; and the truly marvellous boy, who composed a lovely sonata at eight, and Handel, Haydn, and Weber, and their musical congeners, did not satisfy a time craving, not for repose in the Arts, but for excitement. The locomotive, the telegraph, telephones, motor-cars, and the rest aggravated this tendency, and made them long for something stimulating. In music, Meyerbeer did his best to satisfy them, but was not quite equal to the task he set himself. But, the Hour having come, this time the Man also came, a man unquestionably of great genius, but not quite a Mozart, and very different from him, to

Rend with tremendous sound your ears asunder.

Wagner " stimulated " and still stimulates them, as the phrase is, with a vengeance. Mozart is always inspired; that is to say, he does not go in search of musical themes, having no necessity to do so, because they come to him incessantly. Wagner is inspired, and most happily inspired sometimes, but only sometimes, and, where he is not, he ekes out inspiration by astounding craft and ingenuity, and stimulates the ganglionic centres of his worshippers with wave after wave of the same idea slightly altered each time it rises and falls. But I suspect the world generally is getting affannato tanto rather weary of telephones, motor-cars, and other feverish, stimulating appliances, and, if only at week-ends, craves for the tranquillity, shall we say, of a garden. Let that feeling grow, and Mozart, Raphael, and Poets, Sculptors, and Architects akin to them, will come by their own once more. Kings, true kings, always get back their kingdoms."

' You sound," said Veronica, ' a more hopeful note than usually. Do you think that in politics and society, likewise, there are signs of a return to sanity? ' ' Let us hope so," he replied, ' and, in any case, let us be patient, and not make the common mistake of confusing the Passing with the Permanent."

' Meanwhile," said Lamia, ' the mad world, our masters, is not an unamusing performance, so long as one is not obliged to be one of the performers."

Do you remember Veronica once saying of The Garden that I Love, ' The peculiarity of this kitchen-garden is that it contains no vegetables." There was a little ornamental exaggeration in the taunt, but a certain amount of truth underlying it. Where there should have been rows of succulent spinach, there flowered dazzling sweet-williams, homely- smelling lavender where you would naturally have looked for broad beans, and intrusive roses between rows of Scotch kail. There were more sweet than edible peas, and many- coloured pumpkins in lieu of plainer but useful vegetable- marrows. We have gradually changed all that. Not that flowers have been entirely banished from the kitchen- garden, for many- branching sunflowers still tower above breadths of lettuce, and onion-patches are tempered by soaring hollyhocks. But perhaps the most noticeable alteration is the comparatively large space assigned to strawberries. Strawberries, I allow, are not vegetables, but neither are they flowers, and I have never heard Veronica, even in her most culinary moments, say a word against them. Lamia and the Poet, as is the habit of romantic people, are very fond of what that delightful, thoroughly human man of genius, Mr. Barrie, has gracefully christened Little Mary, and get into the finest of frenzies as they glance from bed to bed with the predatory gaze of the full-, grown song-thrush. At the same time they have made several valuable suggestions concerning the prolongation of the strawberry season, and indeed have done everything to the growing of these except contributing one single stroke of honest work, their custom being to reap but not to sow. Lamia has spent many hours, she says, in fathoming the subject, and now has delivered a lecture to me embodying her conclusions.

4 Your earliest crop must be from Royal Sovereign and Laxtons Monarch, by no means ideal strawberries, but as precocious as Mozart, if not so sweet. Furthermore, they must be planted on a gentle slope looking south or south-west, and they must be renewed every two years. They are colossal in size and lavish croppers."

Here she interrupted her discourse by suiting the action to the word, and giving an illustration of her meaning by plunging under the net, and distorting her bow-shaped mouth by putting into it a succulent monster.

' You cannot," she went on, feed these generous bearers too liberally, on much the same principle, I suppose, though I am necessarily rather ignorant in such matters, that I have observed old-fashioned people apply to monthly nurses. Given the above treatment and a proper aspect, these two early bearers will provide you with bowls of fruit for a good fortnight before any others show ripe berries. Your main crop, which will then be quite ready, had better be Sir Joseph Paxton, which will carry you on for a fortnight more, if you have the good sense not to give them all one aspect. Doctor Hogg) the best substitute for British Queen since resembling it in flavour, bearing much more freely, and in every way to be relied on, will by the end of that fortnight be laden with large handsome fruit; and it also, if a certain number of plants be grown in a cool but not overshaded position, will prolong your strawberry season through a fifth week, and in some seasons well into a sixth. Should you, or should you not, grow Waterloo? You shall decide that point for yourself. They are very dark in colour, nearly black outside, and a rich red within, and they ripen later. But they are very soft in texture, and unless they are gathered just at the right moment, creepers and crawlers make way into their heart. Moreover, with the judicious treatment I have told you of, Doctor Hogg can be got to go on bearing large fine-flavoured fruit almost as late as Waterloo. Now, do not suppose I am unacquainted with all the other sorts to be found in Nursery Catalogues. But I wish to save you unnecessary embarrassment, and having delivered this invaluable information I think I am entitled to be elected a Fellow of the Royal Horticultural Society."

' You are one already," I said.

' Am I?" she replied. ' I am so many distinguished things that I had forgotten, perhaps because Veronica pays the subscription for me. I am, as you know, shockingly ignorant of flowers, and I scorn to know anything whatever about vegetables. But in fruit, most of all in consuming and passing an opinion on it, I am an expert. And since Mr. Mallock has explained so lucidly in his enthralling investigation of the most recondite problems of Political Economy that the mind contributes more than the hand to the production of wealth, I will thank you to roll back that net, and this intellectual labourer will have her due share of what I see is underneath it. Could Veronica herself be more practical? And who will now venture to say, if you appropriate the information I have given you, The Garden that I Love is about everything save gardening? '

Thus, thanks to that conflict of opinion that springs from differences of temperament, The Garden that I Love now blends the utile with the dulce, and we are just as self-complacent about our out-door fruit and Jerusalem artichokes as about the oak we did not plant and the roses that were reared in France. Is this egotism? If it be, I think it is pardonable so long as it is not accompanied by unreadiness to remember that there are oaks and roses elsewhere. A belief in one's own swans is an excusable foible, provided it be not accompanied by an assumption that other people have nothing to show but geese. We had an excellent illustration the other day of the generous modesty that inverts that process, and which recognises the superiority of others in respect of a yet more important matter even than gardening. Not a few visitors to the Old Country from the United States honour us by including our home in the range of their sympathetic curiosity; and one of them who was made welcome the other day expatiated in the handsomest manner on the race he regards as his ancestors.

'What strikes me," he said, 'in the folks in these Islands is their enduring vitality and masculine vigour. An old Land it is, and, in a sense, you are an old people. But I think you are, on the whole, the youngest race I know. To use a homely illustration, though you do not talk loudly, you cough and do other kindred things with unequalled violence. Some perhaps would say that it is due to your climate. But in almost everything you display the activity and independence ot youthfulness. You do everything with a certain amount of deliberation, thinking before you act, which some hasty observers mistake for slowness. There is said to be extraordinary strenuousness in my people at home. But you are equally strenuous, though more quietly so. Your boys, and even your girls, take to outdoor games as a duck takes to water. You are not very disciplined, for youth hates discipline. But look at your mental freshness, alike in Science and Literature. I may say it here, though I should have to be cautious in saying it on our side of the water; but I regard it as a remarkable circumstance that, during the two hundred and fifty years of our existence as a separate nation, we have produced some graceful poets and several agreeable men of letters, but not given birth to a Poet in, or anywhere near, the first class. Yet, though you already had your Chaucer, your Spenser, your Shakespeare, your Milton, your Dryden, your Pope, you have had since, and within the last hundred years, your Scott, your Wordsworth, your Byron, your Shelley, your Keats, and your Tennyson. There is no surer sign of youthfulness than the production of fine Poetry; and you are producing it still. I note and confess the fact. Have you, sir," he said, turning pointedly to our Poet, ' any theory on the subject?"

Thus pointedly appealed to, he replied ' Your country has done, and continues to do, so much in this world, and contributes so largely to the sum of human effort, that you can well afford to be as frank and generous as you have shown yourself, and to accept, in good part, what seems to me to be the explanation you are in search of. Your people, as distinct from ourselves, and as a separate nation, were born, so to speak, not young, but in the full flower of manhood. Oddly and, as it seems to me, inaccurately, you are described and still spoken of as a young people. But may I venture to ask if, collectively, and, as a national entity, you ever had any youth? You branched off from these Islands, ready provided, not with the qualities of youth, but with those of meridian manhood, and the tens of thousands from other parts of Europe that seek the hospitality of your shores, are not young but already full-grown. We, meanwhile, with traditional continuity of character and temperament, have retained a certain spirit of youthfulness, or what Wordsworth so beautifully calls " the young lamb's heart amid the grown-up flocks." In the next place, I should say the enduring love of a country life deep-seated in all classes of our people, and their familiarity with hills, streams, woodland, moorland, and sea-shore, have ministered materially to the continued production of poets among us.

Finally, we are an aristocratic people, in the true sense of the word, and what are, to my ears improperly, called the lower classes are the most aristocratic in feeling of all. Now Poetry, as the best flower of Literature, is intellectually aristocratic though sentimentally democratic. By the unceasing arrival of immigrants from all parts of the world, you are, figuratively speaking, perpetually putting water into your wine. We were brewed and racked off long ago, and being rather strong drink, have remained sound to this day. That it may last still longer is my fervent prayer."

And mine also, sir," said our magnanimous guest, and so took farewell.

I could see the Poet was greatly delighted by the foregoing conversation, and in the course of the evening, as we sate under the oak, he reverted to it.

' It was most exhilarating," he said, to hear such a panegyric of England, especially in these days when we hear so much of how precarious is its position, unless it be saved from extinction by what used to be called our Colonies, but that now have grown so self-complacent, thanks to the exaggerated language concerning them employed by some of our own men of Light and Leading, that they describe themselves, and wish to be spoken of, as Sister Nations. Well, names matter but little, provided they do not mislead. But when I remember that, as our American guest of to-day said, England has produced Chaucer, Spenser, Shakespeare, Milton, Dryden, Pope, Wordsworth, Byron, Keats, Shelley, and Tennyson; Bacon, Newton, and Darwin; Marlborough, Nelson, and Wellington; Clive and Warren Hastings; Fielding, Dickens, and Thackeray; that it is England which founded our Indian Empire, and established and still chiefly maintains our Supremacy on the Seas; and when I compare this magnificent and multiform manifestation of genius, capacity, and vigour with what the Sister Nations have as yet contributed to the Empire or mankind, I confess I wax indignant at the flying in the face of incontestable fact, in speaking of " poor little England," and talking of it as though it were the smallest factor in British greatness and power, instead of being, as it really is, the toweringly predominant partner with unlimited responsibility, while all the others, with (at their own wish) a strictly limited liability, contribute a Lilliputian share. I have now liberated my mind, and feel relieved."

What a pity said Lamia, you cannot enunciate such sentiments from a more re-sounding pulpit."

' Use your irresistible influence, Lamia," said Veronica, ' with the reforming Powers-that-Be to procure for the Poet a seat in the Upper Chamber without a Peerage."

I will go about it at once said Lamia; but I am rather afraid lest I should have prepossessed them against me by more than once remarking that of all reforms the one most needed is the reformation of certain Reformers themselves. That is a kind of Charity that I think ought to begin at home, only they seem rather averse from it."

The next day, which was so bright and warm that it led to much sitting out under shady trees, the Poet so far returned to the topic of the previous evening as to say: ' I rather think that, in availing myself of the opportunity so courteously accorded me by our American visitor, I overlooked one influential cause of the persistent production of poetry of high seriousness, to use Matthew Arnold's phrase, among us. You all know the view with which I have long laboured to modify the prevailing opinion that purely lyrical poetry is poetry of the highest order, which it very rarely is, however delightful and seductive may be its quality; since for the greatest poetry Intellect must combine with Feeling, and poetry, genuine poetry, must be born of high thoughts fused and made one with deep emotion. Such in poetry is the highest achievement of all; and the silently meditative and pondering disposition of our race, most conspicuous in the classically educated of them, furnishes the conditions out of which alone great Poets are best evolved. That is the prosaically worded explanation of what I would say, and have said so often. But you know my incorrigible habit of embodying ideas, such as they are, in verse, and as I have not yet written down nor dictated to Lamia a sonnet that came to me this morning on that theme, I will, if you like, try to recall it."

Lamia, who seems to think that somehow or other her co-operation is needed on such occasions, moved closer to him and took his hand in hers. Thus assisted he recited:

GREAT NUPTIALS

Now for great nuptials let the bells be rung,
And immemorial symphonies resound,
From high-groined roof time-tattered bannerets hung,
And flowers round porch and pillar wreathed and wound,

For Soul with Mind is coming to be wed, Feeling with Intellect to seal its troth, Inseparable bond twixt heart and head, With hierarch Wisdom dominating both. A splendid offspring shall from them be born, Poetry, first and noblest of the breed, Sculpture, and Song, and Painting, to adorn Cathedrals open unto every Creed: Race that shall never older grow than now, But wear eternal youth upon their brow.

October. It always seems to me that the most pathetic month of the year is October; for, so it be windless and sunny, which it usually is in our part of the world, the beauty of one's garden is of rich matronly mellowness and distinction. But the Damoclean sword of Winter hangs over its head, and no one knows when the Fates will cut the cord, and let the sharp frosty blade fall upon the predestined victim, as it awaits, in stationariness, the descent of doom. Legends are the gradual growth of kindly imagination; and I will not pledge myself to the absolute accuracy of the following. But Veronica often tells how the Poet, when once allowed to occupy the out-door bedroom, whose origin and advantages I trust you remember, rising in the middle of the night to saunter in the Garden, since the full moon was smiling sweetly on every bank, suspected the intentions of that fascinating female luminary, and that she would, when she saw the sun was coming, blight all its posies with a chilling frost. Thereupon, he carried out from his bedroom every chair that was in it, placed them round about the beds containing the most tender things, and then stretched all the newspapers he could lay his hands on in the adjoining lumber-room, then his dressing-gown, and finally his quilt, and some say the sheets over these again, and prolonged the existence of the fragile for some time. For the noticeable thing about October frosts is that they often come with the dawn just once, play the mischief, and then do not recur for several weeks:

Now we have been taught by experience, and the idee mere attributed to the Poet has by gradual evolution given birth to cunningly adjusted gauze and tiffany, after going through a period of the bitterest controversy with the Maids, in consequence of the Poet, to whom, I really don't know why, they always give in at last, over their dust-sheets, which he declared were just the thing for sheltering the flower-beds against an early solitary frost, while they, on the contrary, maintained that their precious coverings were being ruined. Finally, Veronica, overhearing the Poet pleading in his most persuasive manner, ' Oh, but you'll let me have them!" said, Have what?"

Then the dreadful truth came out; and Lamia, pretending, in order to shield him, that the idea had proceeded from her, got a serious lecture for her wasteful frivolity; and the dust-sheets were withdrawn into private life. Then Lamia came to the rescue.

' Who she asked, is thepremiere danseuse just now, at those Palaces I once went to with the Poet? I will write to her, unless' turning to me ' you prefer to write to her yourself, and ask her where she gets all those short but delicate gossamer flounces that satisfy the Lord Chamberlain and Censor of Plays and Morals; and then she perhaps will send us furlongs of it to dance and swing in the wind, with all the innocence of our blameless rural life."

' I cannot help saying to myself sometimes," observed the Poet this morning, What an uneventful and unromantic life people must have had to read the novels they seem to peruse with such eager curiosity. I am not alluding to novels of adventure like, say, A Gentleman of France or Les

Trois Mousquetaires, for we none of us can well have had, in these days, quite such captivating experiences as they describe. I am alluding to novels the bulk of those published the theme of which is Elk et Lui, Elle et Moi, or Moi et Lui. I cannot help feeling sorry for such readers, that their days have been so utterly destitute of amiable episodes as to render the reading of vicarious romance so enthralling. Nor am I thinking of the novels, far too numerous of late, in which the supposed romance in them is the very opposite of romantic; being wholly sensual, and sometimes revolting. It is a pity there is no longer a common hangman to burn such outrages on masculine dignity and feminine delicacy. That, by the way. But what I would point out is, that romantic experiences between human beings cease to be romantic, when narrated realistically in prose, or indeed in prose at all, since they require, for the communication of them to others, the intensifying imaginative magic of Poetry. Just think of Romeo and Juliet or As Tou Like It fading into the common light of day by being turned into a novel! Imagine but alas! it has been done Dante's terse but all-sufficing recital of the love-tragedy of Francesca de Rimini, degraded into a spun-out stage-play for the delectation of the groundlings! That indeed is enough to make the angels weep. But can such fantastic tricks be evidence of human progress, of which we hear so much?

The trashiest novels have ousted and replaced the noblest poems in the affections of nine out of ten readers of to-day. To state that fact is to brand the Age with mental deterioration and spiritual eclipse. Thank heaven! into the Garden that we love that poison has not penetrated."

' Fit audience, though few," murmured Veronica, with her inexhaustible generous optimism. There are, and there always will be, readers and loving readers of Poetry, though it may seem to be dethroned from its ancient place in the affection among mankind at large. I think I have heard you say that the inferior will, if left free to choose, always prefer the inferior, in other words what is most congenial to them. In old days, Authority used to say, read this, read that; and the revered advice was obeyed. In these days, Authority is extinct; and critics' judgment, for the most part, humours and follows the majority, otherwise the inferior, instead of trying to instruct their choice, and direct their taste. Hence,

Literature nowadays means, and is synonymous with, Novels. Yet let us not forget your distinction between the Passing and the Permanent. Novels vanish, poems endure. Of Poetry we may say, Thou art always the self-same, and thy years shall not fail."

Lamia had listened intently to all the foregoing, but contributed no word, either playful or serious to it. But when Veronica ceased, she took the Poet's hand more timidly than usual, and, while a slight and most becoming colour came into her cheeks, said: I wrote some verses this morning, which 1 am sure are not poetry, though they were sincerely felt while I did so."

' Do let us hear them," said Veronica.

Yes, do indeed," echoed the Poet and myself.

Whereupon, with yet heightened colour, she recited:

Awake! awake!

For the merle in the brake Is louder and louder singing; Arise! arise! The lark in the skies Is heavenward wheeling and winging. The dew of the dawn is on leaf and lawn,

And gleams on the blushing roses;

Haste, haste, as so oft, ere in copse and croft The nightingale's nocturn closes.

Would you have her not wait at the garden gate,

Where she trembles, but longs to meet you, And with crimsoning cheek like a snow-tipped peak,

She will hold out her hand to greet you? Then away, away, through the love-long day,

O'er meadow, and wood, and heather; You may roam where you will, through the vale, up the hill,

Together, and still together.

That is all; for there it stopped."

' It was about time it did," said Veronica smilingly. But the lines are very musical."

Yes," said the Poet.

They are very musical," said Veronica. As for me, I thought them beautiful beyond words.

' Yes," said the Poet; c they have music, and, I almost think, poetry in them, even if, dear, it be lyrical poetry of a perhaps rudimentary kind. But what I also notice, and what pleases me in them, is the evidence they give of the plasticity of the English language, which, I once heard an erudite German philologist say, he being familiar with almost every tongue and every literature, he believed to be one of the causes of the continuous superiority of English poetry for six hundred years. A poet, of adequate craft, can do pretty much what he likes with it. The supreme master, modern master at least, in this respect, is Byron, who could write:

The desolator desolate,

The victor overthrown, The arbiter of others' fate

A suppliant for his own, and in The Isles of Greece and The Army of Sennacherib Nebuchadnezzar, and numbers of other lyrical poems, exhibits and maintains this dominating directness of diction, written as if with electric instantaneousness.

I am glad," said Lamia modestly, I read my poor little verses, since they have elicited your commentary."

But I say, as for me, I preferred the verses themselves, and shall ask for a copy of them.

Occasionally Lamia admits us all to the innermost sanctuary of her real feelings; and she did so this afternoon, when we had finished tea under the now wide-spreading tulip-tree. A song-thrush hard by, suddenly, as is the wont with his tuneful tribe, burst into a passing reminiscence of his amorous vernal notes; and Lamia, quite forgetful of the prosaic reasons she had adduced as to the real cause of their trilling and gurgling, said, in her deepest and richest tone

May I recite " The Deeper Note "? '

The Poet remained silent, but Veronica replied ' Yes, do, dear!"

Thereupon, with variations of inflection outvying every merle or mavis that ever enchanted the woodlands, she recited to us as follows:

THE DEEPER NOTE i Birds of victorious Spring,

Through sunshine and through rain Sing, sing, sing,

Reiterate the strain; To you life doth not bring Sadness or pain.

ii Your unforeboding song,

With each returning year, Is just as sweet and strong,

As silvery and clear, As when the Attic throng

Stood, husht, to hear.

in Yet something do you miss

Of what to us is lent; The spiritual bliss,

The whispered message sent From unseen world to this,

For our admonishment:

The mystery half-divined

Of ' Where," when we depart,

Leaving our loved behind Alone to bear the smart,

High melodies of mind, Deep music of the heart.

v So would I not exchange

For your my graver lot, The wider reach and range

Of feelings you have not, Experience rich and strange,

And fondness unforgot.

With the last word she rose, and walked slowly away, for I suspect she was near to breaking down.

Shortly I said: 4 What a blessed day it was we made The Garden that I Love."

Yes," added the Poet, ' and, still more, when Lamia came into it."

Printed by R. R. CLARK, LIMITED, Edinburgh.

THE PROSE WORKS OF THE POET LAUREATE

THE GARDEN THAT I LOVE

Extra Crown vo. Illustrated. 6s.

SATURDA Y REVIEW. " In this sunshiny book with the Tennysonian title, Mr. Alfred Austin makes a charming addition to the literature of the English garden."

SPEAKER. " The Garden that I Love is pure delight. The sense of what Milton termed ' retired leisure' is in the book, and with it the scent of the flowers and much quick appreciation of country sights and sounds."

THE GARDEN THAT I LOVE

SECOND SERIES. Extra Crown Svo.

IN VERONICA'S GARDEN

Extra Crown 8vo. Illustrated. 6s.

BLACKWOOUS MAGAZINE. " Mr. Austin leads us back in his delightful way into the garden which we all love. It is just the book to lie in the embrasure of the window looking out upon a garden full of tangled sweetness, where lilies have lifted their tall heads and roses blown from the beginning of time."

DAILY NEWS. "Mr. Alfred Austin in Veronica's Garden continues his praises of The Garden that I Love. White, of Selbome, was not more precise than is Mr. Austin in noting the advent and ways of the blossoms and birds, or in observing the wayward, laggard or hurrying steps of the season."

LAMIA'S WINTER QUARTERS

Extra Crown 8v0. Illustrated. 6s. Presentation Edition. Cloth gilt. I CM. 6d.

ST. JAMES'S GAZETTE. "from the poetical 'Invocation' addressed to the Queen, with which the book begins, to the lyric, ' Good Night," with which it ends, the volume is charming. We have here all Mr. Austin's suavity of diction and delicacy of sentiment, the artistic pleasure in the beautiful, the true poet's delight in Italy, which, taken together, make a piece of prose, which, in its way. is as near perfect as may be."

DAILY TELEGRAPH. "We are never bored throughout all these delightful pages. We live on a level of distinguished thoughts, expressed with elegance and refinement."

HAUNTS OF ANCIENT PEACE

Extra Crown vo. Illustrated. 6s.

DAILY TELEGRAPH. " A charmingly conceived and charmingly executed book, which will be read with delight by all who admire the delicate graces of the Poet Laureate's prose style."

DAILY NEWS. " A delightful wander-book. Breezy and redolent of country charm. Under its spell we lose for a time the brick-and-mortar civilisation that sometimes seems all-pervading, and gladly fly with the writer and his three friends to the green lanes and fields outside our prison."

THE POET'S DIARY

Edited by LAMIA. Extra Crown 8vo. js. 6d.

ST. JAMES'S GAZETTE. "Always instinct with a true and discriminating appreciation of what is beautiful in art and nature, full of a scholarship which brings an agreeable taste of older days, and written with grace and wit. There is a very real charm for the traveller who can appreciate another's great love for Rome and Italy, and for the reader who likes the taste of Lamb or Hazlitt and the older essayists on his palate."

STANDARD. "Mi. Alfred Austin's prose fantasies are always welcome. A most pleasing medley of reminiscence, observation, and genial philosophy."

MACMILLAN AND CO., LTD., LONDON.

THE POETICAL WORKS OF THE POET LAUREATE

New and Cheaper Edition. Crown vo. 2s. net.

THE DOOR OF HUMILITY

THE SEASON: A Satire. Crown 8vo. 55. THE GOLDEN AGE: A Satire. Crown 8vo. 55. MADONNA'S CHILD. Fcap. 8vo. 2s. 6d. net.

THE TOWER OF BABEL: A Celestial Love Drama. Crown 8vo. 53.

THE HUMAN TRAGEDY. Crown 8vo. 55. SAVONAROLA: A Tragedy. Crown 8vo. 53. LYRICAL POEMS. Crown 8vo. 53. NARRATIVE POEMS. Crown 8vo. 53. ENGLISH LYRICS. Crown 8vo. 33. 6d. PRINCE LUCIFER. Crown 8vo. 55. FORTUNATUS THE PESSIMIST. (Out of Print.)

AT THE GATE OF THE CONVENT, and other Poems. Crown 8vo. 6s.

ALFRED THE GREAT: England's Darling. Crown 8vo. as. 6d. net.

THE CONVERSION OF WINCKELMANN, and other Poems. Crown 8vo. 55.

A TALE OF TRUE LOVE, and other Poems. Crown 8vo. 53.

FLODDEN FIELD: A Tragedy. Crown 8vo. 43. 6d. net. ROME OR DEATH. Crown 410. gs. VICTORIA. 8vo. 6d net

SONGS OF ENGLAND. Enlarged Edition. Fcap. 8vo. is. net.

MACMILLAN AND CO., LTD., LONDON.

Lightning Source UK Ltd.
Milton Keynes UK
03 November 2010